PUT *Passion* FIRST

Why *Sexual Chemistry* Is the Key to Finding and Keeping Lasting Love

CAROL CASSELL, Ph.D.

New York Chicago San Francisco Lisbon London Madrid Mexico City
Milan New Delhi San Juan Seoul Singapore Sydney Toronto

Library of Congress Cataloging-in-Publication Data

Cassell, Carol, 1936–
    Put passion first : why sexual chemistry is the key to finding and keeping lasting
love / Carol Cassell.
        p.   cm.
    ISBN 978-0-07-149264-5 (alk. paper)
    1. Women —Psychology.   2. Women —Conduct of life.   3. Self-realization in
women.   I. Title.

HQ1206.C29   2007
646.7'7082—dc22   2007027209

1 2 3 4 5 6 7 8 9 0   FGR/FGR   0 9 8 7

ISBN 978-0-07-149264-5
MHID   0-07-149264-X

McGraw-Hill books are available at special quantity discounts to use as premiums and
sales promotions, or for use in corporate training programs. For more information, please
write to the Director of Special Sales, Professional Publishing, McGraw-Hill, Two Penn
Plaza, New York, NY 10121-2298. Or contact your local bookstore.

This book is printed on acid-free paper.

*This book is dedicated to the not-so-little tribe
I belong to: Cassell, Mendez, Kauffman, Miller—
specifically, Bob Cassell, my kids (Don, Alisa, John,
Michael, Emily, and Lisa), my six grandkids (Justin,
Max, Aurora Ann, Joshua, Jacob, and Ian), my
brothers (Tom, John, and Phil), and my many nieces
and nephews, plus the in-laws and the out-laws
(Jessica, Karen, Helen, Mary, Greg, and Roxanne)—
indeed, through thick or thin, we are family.*

Contents

Acknowledgments

This book was not written on an isolated island—I couldn't have done it alone. It was shaped over time from many conversations with countless numbers of people. Unfortunately, it is only possible to identify and thank just a few of those who helped transform my thoughts to these pages.

My gratitude to Linda Konner, my literary agent, not only for representing me so well but for her straightforward and spot-on advice. And my appreciation to Johanna Bowman, my editor, for her enthusiasm and her finely honed editing as well as for her warmth and gentle way of steering me onto the right path. I also thank Jonathan Dolger for his longtime support and for his reviews of earlier renditions.

A special note of appreciation to three very special people for reviewing every page of this book (including revisions!): most especially to Bob Cassell for his rock-solid loving support and his skills with syntax and grammar; to Linda Penaloza for her keen editing eye and graceful insights; and to my brother, Phil Miller, for his creative, artistic energy and sense of humor that made this book more readable and great fun to talk about.

To my friends and colleagues who generously gave of their time—in interviews and in offering advice about this book-in-progress—I offer thanks: Mary Dillon, Leslie Trickey, Stella Resnick, Alan Kishbaugh, Kay Scott, Sol Gordon, John Richardson, Phillip Gibbs, Kay Scott, and Gina Ogden. Especially to my "Artist's Way" writing pals, Tara Lumpkin, Linda Moscarella, and Marie-Rose Phan-Le. I also offer thanks to my colleagues in the Society for the Scientific Study of Sexuality, particularly the western region, for their scholarship and camaraderie.

My endearing gratitude to Judith Rinehart for her priceless editorial assistance and friendship. Thanks so much, Judith.

My appreciation to Tim Lannan, one of my most valued friends, who always crystallizes hazy concepts and nudges me to write from the heart. And my heartfelt thanks for his immeasurable contributions to Jon Hendershott, a passionate man and a top-notch journalist who helped shape the tone and the content of this book.

Lastly, I thank the women and men who graciously shared their personal experiences with me and offered such sound "lessons learned" advice. They appear disguised in these pages, under fictitious names, but their contributions enriched this book tenfold.

Introduction

The Promise of This Book

If I cautioned you that by climbing a certain mountain you'd have a fifty-fifty chance of having an accident—one that could affect you emotionally and economically for many years—would you do it? Despite the dire warnings of breakup danger ahead, most of us at some point in our lives just lace up our hiking shoes and head for the marital summit.

Consider the odds. The next clock, blender, or DVD player you give as a wedding gift is likely to last longer than the marriage; the success rate for marriage is the statistical equivalent of a coin toss. Close to half of first marriages end in divorce; 60 percent of second marriages fail. And there has been a recent spike in divorces among older couples, dubbed "the thirty-seven-year itch." The number of live-in lovers who break up every year is anyone's guess, but most of us know at least one such couple.

What makes statistics and personal stories of failed love even more disturbing is that many counselors offer only eat-your-peas advice to women to soldier on in fixer-upper relationships while writers dish out quickie recipes for "finding your soul mate." Few offer nitty-gritty insight into how women can stop falling into a tangle of disappointing or disintegrating relationships.

In stark contrast, here in *Put Passion First* you will find an unadorned explanation of what is causing this discontent. Would you believe it's not about a lack of sensitive, compatible, caring romantic love? It's not. It's about a lack of a *passionate* love in women's lives.

Why don't we know this?

The problem is that the airwaves, the Internet, and books from self-help to scholarly are full of advice telling us that the heat of "sexual chemistry" as the raison d'être for a relationship doesn't measure up to "True Love"—that sure and steady relationship. Or they repeatedly warn of the danger in going overboard with passion, because it is nothing more than a thinly veiled impulse—lust, that chameleon of love's sexual desires. Or they caution us to avoid, as Johnny Cash and June Carter sang, getting "married in a fever hotter than a pepper sprout," because, according to the naysayers, if you do you can forget about getting that anniversary diamond necklace.

Ironically this belief about compatibility as the red carpet leading to a lasting relationship is popular in both folk psychology and scientific psychology, even though the scant research evidence isn't persuasive. Still there is no dearth of marriage counselors and advice columnists telling us not to judge the potential of a relationship that lacks sexual chemistry too harshly, because sex is not the be-all and end-all of living happy ever after. Mostly they predict being good buddies will trump passion, because they believe sex is the first thing to go after you see him night after night in his faded Boy Scout skivvies.

But they are misguided or just plain wrong.

What is overlooked and undervalued is *passion*. Passion is that intangible and potent fusion between the *sizzle* of sexual chemistry and the calmer, loving feelings of being emotionally connected to your partner.

The fact that passion is intangible and somewhat ineffable has left too many advice givers with blinders on, unable to see that passion is so essential to our hearts and souls that we will walk over hot coals to have it. I'm not saying that being comfortable with your partner and sharing values and goals for your future together isn't important. Of course it is. But being passionately wild for each other is just as crucial as emotional compatibility and the rest of the items on mate-matching checklists, like agreeing about how many kids you would like to have. When a love partnership begins with a strong initial sexual attraction and then evolves into a passionate intimacy, you are more likely to maintain romantic love's unique intoxicating emotions as you travel over the changing hills and valleys of a committed relationship than if all you have is compatibility.

Matchmaker, Matchmaker, Make Me a Match?

The reality that without the spark of sexual chemistry a romantic match won't be lit is getting some attention among the Internet matchmakers. They finally recognize that while single people want a compatible partner, most don't want it at the expense of being sexually tuned in to each other. The cyberspace matchmakers aren't planning to change their compatibility-mating process but admit to searching for the ultimate sexy soul mate model—a scientifically inspired match based on compatible personality traits *and* mutual sexual chemistry.

But it's no slam dunk. For example, Pepper Schwartz, a sociologist well known for her research into couples' relationships who is the science adviser for Perfectmatch.com, says she recognizes, despite the upside to computer matching, that technology isn't likely to replace the mystery of who will light whose fire. Still, she believes it makes sense to try Internet matching: "What this does is try to narrow it down so you spend less time with people who are totally out of the question. We're just upping your chances."

Helen Fisher, an anthropologist at Rutgers University, is the resident science guru at Chemistry.com. She agrees with Schwartz's assessment that matches made in cyberspace can be dicey. Fisher acknowledges that what appears to be a great match given background, intelligence, aspirations, and the hormones of sexual personality can fall apart when two people meet in person. And that is why, despite the pluses of computerized matchmaking, she believes a match comes from a "constellation of factors, including sex drive, romantic love, and a range of factors that helps us form an attachment." It is that "constellation of factors" that the computer can't pin down.

Despite the popularity and impressive marriage track records of the Internet e-yentas, it is a mistake to pin all of your wishful hopes for a partner on a formula of harmonious compatibility. Even if it is backed by a computerized wild card played in the chance you will be sexually attracted to each other, it is an online match. What happens between two people is still more magic than science.

In the long run, denying or ignoring your yearning for a passionate, sensual love doesn't work. Faking your feelings or pretending that it doesn't matter is disastrous for a relationship in every way. Eventually the lack of sensual pleasure erodes the quality of the partnership and leads to frustration and disappointment, even despair, and often to divorce.

Sexual Cravings

The depth of women's craving for passionate love crystallized for me at one of my seminars. I was reading Wendy Lee's "Lover's Duet" from the book *Passionate Hearts* to make my point that passionate love is deeper and far more complex than either sex or love alone or combined:

> *What began as an urge to satisfy*
> *something primal in me,*
> *became a desire to unite deeply*
> *with you.*
> *I rose in love to your touch.*
> *I lost myself in the fullness of your kiss,*
> *the silky glide of your arms, the strong harbor of your*
> *   thighs,*
> *The heat of your body*
> *inside mine. . . .*

When I finished, I looked up in a room full of women so quiet they appeared to have stopped breathing.

After the workshop, women came up to me one after another and expressed a hungry longing to experience more erotic passion in their lives. Yet in the same breath they expressed a sense of unease about the seductive power of passion and how it could make them vulnerable to an unhealthy or chaotic relationship.

What I learned from the women there, and from many, many other women later, is that women have a deep yearning to have more passion in their lives. But they aren't getting what they crave because they are stuck in an emotional gridlock that has become an invisible but formidable barrier. Too many women are either fearful of or ambivalent about allowing themselves to jump into the deep end of passionate love.

Listening to those many voices talking about their profound yearning for passion and love—commingled with their uneasiness—spurred me to write this book to help women overcome their self-defeating barriers to finding and loving the sensual partner they crave.

Passion and Friendship: The Best of Two Worlds

For more than thirty-five years, through my books, writings, workshops, and seminars, I've dedicated my life to achieving a deeper understanding of the dynamics between women and men and their experiences with intimate relationships. I've learned a lot about the power of passionate love and its ability to add intense joy to life and its uncanny, bewildering power to disappear in a heartbeat. And I've had more than my fair share of feeling the dizziness of passionate love and suffering the gut-wrenching pangs of heartbrokenness when it fizzled.

In a nutshell, my research into how we make decisions about love and sex and how we deal with loving and sensual relationships has set the stage for me to help you embark on a journey to find a passionate love, one that will stand the test of time. My premise is simply this: if you have a comfortable, compatible love but not passion, you don't have enough. If you have sexual heat but not friendship, you don't have enough. Neither lust nor love by itself is enough. It is actually pretty simple: if you aren't sexually in lust and if you aren't tickled when in his company, he's not for you no matter how well you "get along." It has become clear to me that too many women and men settle for less and end up missing being loved the way they would have loved being loved.

I believe that a passionate partnership offers you the best of all worlds because it combines two separate but equally important elements—sensual heat and friendship. At one level, it powers the mysterious energy and intimacy of falling in love. And at the same time, it has the same capacity for standing the test of time as a relationship in which two people are partners and friends as well as lovers.

What Passion Is and Isn't

My definition of *passionate love* isn't the fairy-tale rendition of romantic love where everything is always coming up roses. A passionate love isn't a free pass around the relationship board. A couple may love each other passionately, but they still will have to overcome the challenges of being a couple, and sometimes they will have to walk on eggshells to keep the peace. Passionately loving each other means that you mutually care for each other's well-being, that you are interested in each other as individuals, and that you are both committed to making your relationship bloom and grow. Then there's the icing on the lovin' cake: you are erotically drawn to each other by an inevitable and seemingly magical connection.

The Road Map

In this book you'll find a relationship road map marking where the scenery is worth a longer look, where you might want to stop and check out the possibilities, and how to overcome detours, gridlock, and unexpected potholes to get you where you want to be. At every step along the way I'll encourage you to give yourself permission to aim for the kind of love that is, at its core, a sensual love partnership. You may be seeking to find a partner. Or you may be at the beginning of a promising relationship. Or you may be in a settled relationship and want it to be more.

No matter your situation, you will find practical and doable ways to overcome the prickly problems a woman faces in trying to sort out the sex–passion–love–soul mate equation, such as considering how to:

- Take off the emotional blinders to get a clearer look into how your emotions, expectations, and behaviors may be keeping you from having the relationship you need and desire
- Accept the way a man expresses his emotions about sex and love, not the way you would like him to
- Allow yourself to embrace a romantic or a sexual experience for whatever it is—with enthusiasm and a willingness to enjoy wherever it takes you

- Stop making the same mistakes about falling in love with the wrong men for all the wrong reasons
- Avoid being too quick to shut out the possibilities of a relationship and allow for passion to grow, even though you aren't initially all that sexually turned on to him
- Communicate your need for a sexual and emotional connection without being demanding or threatening
- Deal with the snags and the realities—the need for breathing space and boundaries, the dark emotions of jealousy, or the temptation to stray—that creep into the bedroom and can ruin your relationship

This isn't a book about how to pour on the charm and entrap a guy or how to pull his emotional or horny strings to get him to desire us or how to get him to march up the aisle to the beat of our drums. This book *is* about reclaiming your birthright to be juicy, sensual, erotic women, celebrating your built-in capacity for intimacy and allowing yourself to dance to the pure joy of being passionately in love.

How This Book Is Put Together

I know you can cultivate a deeper understanding of passionate love, and at the same time begin to experience greater intimacy in your relationships, by putting science to work for you. Because what is genuine and real is more fascinating than fairy tale–infused romantic fiction, I've built this book on solid theoretical ground. This ground holds the bittersweet truths I've uncovered from research studies—my own efforts and many others—about sexual attraction, sexual compatibility or lack thereof, and the many pleasures and sometimes heartaches of being passionately in love.

Some people worry that looking at love and intimacy through the cool rational lens of science could extinguish the heated fires of romance. But that's not true. A clear-eyed look at love doesn't demolish the beauty of passion or negate its profound impact on our lives. Galileo's scientific explanation of the universe doesn't ruin the moment; it makes it more interesting.

Like my fellow social scientists, I'm gratified by the dazzling amount of research about men and women's relationships that has helped us learn more about the meaning of love and sex in our lives. But I've found it challenging to make sense of the conflicts among the many theories about love. Go to the psychological literature for a clue about love and you will find it variously described as an irrational compulsion, a neurosis, an emotional storm, or an immature ideal. Tune in to the psychoanalytic point of view and you'll hear that adult relationships are reflections of childhood relationships—a replay of old Mommy and Daddy scripts. Ask other theorists about love and you'll be told that love depends more on being likable than on being lovable. The behaviorists are sure that love is a rational exchange in which couples negotiate deals based on their needs and asserting that power—whether measured in dollars, beauty, or brawn—is the ultimate aphrodisiac. Anthropologists bring to light buried imprints of culture that show up in our modern love stories, such as our need to "pair-bond" in one way or another. Sociobiologists look deep inside human biology to explain that our romantic passions are the product of brain mechanisms.

To be blunt, most of the analytic language is so polysyllabic or obtuse that a decoding ring is needed to translate the work into plain English. Clues about the power and meaning of passionate love are in there somewhere, but all we are left with is a smudged fingerprint. I've gotten rid of the jargon to allow you to peek behind the research curtains into the lives of other women (and men)—not only what they say about love and sex but also how they actually behave.

The Stories Behind the Studies

Going beyond the research-based studies to learn more about the power of passion in love relationships, I developed a "Passionate Love Survey" and began by handing it out to people attending my presentations or workshops. (I still offer the survey on my website, carolcassell.com. Please do visit, fill it out, and get it back to me!) Even when my presentations were about my work at the Centers for Disease Control and Prevention—prevention of teen pregnancy—discussions, particularly the after-sessions, turned into talking about personal expectations and experiences about love and sex and relationships.

I soon discovered that no topic interests people as much as love and sex, and most, given the opportunity, are willing to talk about their relationships—past, present, and hopes for the future. I also learned that when people see you as a nonjudgmental researcher and expert on topics related to sexuality, they become comfortable telling you anything—much more than they'll tell friends and in some cases their partners. I've lost count of the number of people I have spoken with, either individually or in group discussions; some were colleagues, some were acquaintances or friends of friends (my policy is not to interview friends), and some were complete strangers. The interviews—most planned, some spontaneous—were conducted over a span of four years and in different settings from conference meeting rooms to offices to coffee shops. I especially recall an unexpected and enlightening discussion about how being passionately in love with each other makes all the difference when things get tough—like getting downsized on a job or if an illness strikes—with a woman I met on a plane headed for Clearwater, Florida.

People's stories never fail to fascinate and to offer advice worth sharing. Therefore, throughout the book, I've blended women's and men's personal stories and points of views, along with my own experiences—both professional and personal—to put more flesh on the research bones.

Are Men from Mars and Women from Venus?

I realize that not all men or all women think and act alike, but for ease in writing and reading I refer to *men* and *women* as a form of shorthand. When I say "men" or "women" do or don't do something, I don't men *all* men or *all* women. I am referring to most men or most women, based on the findings of research studies indicating that a majority of men or women feel or behave in a certain way. If the research findings indicate less than a majority, I say *some*.

Differences between men and women are real, but keep in mind that the distribution of their interests and behaviors in love and sex take the form of what researchers call "overlapping normal curves." In short, men and women are more similar than different on many of the dimensions of the topics I talk about in this book. Thus, we can safely conclude that men are not from Mars and women are not from Venus; they are, perhaps, from North and South Carolina.

Be Ready for Him to Come A-Knockin' at Your Door

As you follow the pathways laid out in this book, you will find yourself gaining greater insight into your unique wild-at-heart nature. You'll become more at ease about expressing your playful, womanly, sexy self and less likely to deny it or not acknowledge it.

As you become less timid about unmasking who you really are, you'll find yourself choosing a partner with a more confident heart. And in the meantime, you'll be less likely to get bogged down in a Drama Queen's desperation for the universe to provide you with a soul mate *now*, before you get too old to enjoy him.

As a confident, sensual, passionate woman, you are more likely to find the kind of man who sees and loves you for who you are. Most of all, you'll be ready to answer when a passionate love comes a-knockin' at your door.

What Is Passion?

1

Why You Crave and Need Passionate Love

I *drowned in the fire of having you; I burned in the river of not having you.* As a woman, you yearn to feel with every fiber of your being the fire of a passionate love—that erotic, sensual, vulnerable, volatile, euphoric emotion that hijacks the soul, the mind, and the body. Being passionately in love rocks your world like nothing else. The irrepressible power of passion connects you to a sensual and loving man in a way that is sexy, gritty, and full of risks, good times, and bad timing and feels like you have found a pot of gold at the end of the love rainbow.

Years ago, on a tiny piece of paper I still carry in my wallet, I wrote a quote: "I drowned in the fire of having you; I burned in the river of not having you." I know that quote makes no literal sense, but it makes perfect sense to anyone who has passionately loved another person. What makes passionate love so thrilling and so scary—all at the same time—is that it taps into the hidden forces within you, your lust for erotic sensations, your desire for the touch of skin, and your need for the sweetness of intimacy.

Getting What You Crave

Why aren't you getting the passionate love you crave? What I've discovered in talking with countless men and women about love, sex, and passion is that, while our sexually obsessed culture feeds us a steady diet of sexual imagery, most women are starved when it comes to understanding and expressing their true sensual nature and deeply felt passion.

Then, at every turn, you are bombarded with messages about the importance of finding a harmonious, compatible partner for love to "last." Most of us grew up being taught that a good marriage is built on the bedrock of mutual respect, commitment to staying together, devotion to each other, and ability to communicate. It's not that these aren't worthy qualities of a "good" marriage; they are. But those qualities of a pillar of society—a blue-ribbon-winning marriage—are not enough for deep-in-your-bones satisfaction with being together, and many married people know it. Even if neither spouse can pinpoint what is missing, they feel it.

The problem, as I have said before, is that the conventional wisdom—from everyone from your aunt Sophie to the Internet matchmakers who have staked their success on the idea that lasting love is based on compatibility—is dead wrong. And love advice from columnists and marriage therapists is off the mark. While compatibility is a player in long-term relationships, it isn't the only player or the most valuable player. If you have a comfortable, compatible love without sexual sparks, you don't have enough. If you have sexual heat but not friendship, you don't have enough.

Neither lust nor love by itself is enough. You have to have passion.

This may seem obvious, but it's amazing how many women downplay their erotic desires in their search for a soul mate because they want to believe that having comfort, security, and companionship in a relationship will be enough. And it isn't.

Scratch the surface of a contented couple and you'll find that the sexual passion is always there—it ebbs and flows, but it can ignite in a heartbeat. Passion is ultimately the glue that makes a partnership exciting and playful and helps it stick.

To take you farther down the road to having the passionate love you desire, in this chapter you'll learn more about how your emotions change through the phases of sexual attraction to a deeper bonding and why matchmaking that ignores sexual chemistry rarely sparks a fire. Most of all, you will explore why our cravings for a passionate love are so compelling that even if we get burned by the hot flame of love's passion we are drawn back to the fire, over and over again.

Why Passion Matters

You go to a party, meet a man, and discover you have everything in common from politics to faith to what you would do if you won the lottery. Still, nothing "sizzles"—that quicksilver feeling of sexual attraction is not there. Don't be too quick to brush aside the absence of that mysterious force, because that is a huge "not there."

If you rate sexual attraction on a scale of one to ten—where ten equals "I want to rip his pants off," five equals "whatever," and one equals "nada"—you need to have at least a six (better yet, an eight) before pursuing any relationship. With real effort and a lot of luck, you might be able to turn the heat up a notch, but because so much is involved in sexual passion it's hard to do more than that.

Still, you don't initially always have to be hit with a lightning bolt—breathtaking passionate relationships have grown from being "just friends." And lust has been known to trigger romance and visa versa. But you have to feel sexually drawn to him—if not instantly, then definitely before you consider exchanging keys or choosing the china pattern.

The Chain Reaction

What sets off a chain reaction of falling passionately in love is an inexplicable magnetism—an invisible force, like electricity: sexual chemistry. You can't see it, you can't touch it, you can't smell it; you recognize it by how it affects you.

Marie, a woman in her early forties, tells me how she fell passionately in love, at the wrong time and against all of her better judgment: "I had no intention of getting married. I had just graduated from college, moved to Washington, DC, gotten a great job, and was looking forward to being a single wild woman dancing the nights away at trendy bars. Mostly, because I came from a small town and a small college, I wanted to experience what sex would be like with different types of men—short ones, tall ones, a man with a beard or a mustache, and so on. I wanted to spread my wings, take a bite out of life.

"I noticed him sitting in the patio area of a coffee shop, because he was—no way to make nice—a dorky-looking guy with an odd haircut, wearing a thrift-store jacket, and shuffling papers out of a beat-up vintage briefcase. I sat down at a table and took out a book. Without a word, he got up from his table and sat down at mine. Hey, that's way too cheeky, I remember thinking. He asked me what I was reading. A light rain began, but we just sat there and talked. I could feel myself acting giddy. I knew something was happening, and it *was* something. I called my girlfriend and told her about him—how we didn't have much in common besides admiring street artists. Besides, he was a computer wizard and a poet, and I don't get either computers or poetry. 'He is the one!' she said. 'Cool it. This isn't eighth grade' was all I could say; but I was busted. I knew I had to marry him, because I would never be able to marry anyone else.

"He isn't the kind of man you can easily picture as a husband. And I still don't picture myself as a wifely kind of person. Marriage is so much better, and at times so much worse, than I ever thought it could be. I passionately love him, and, thank God—even after twenty years—he loves me passionately back."

She laughs, and adds, "Who knew Prince Charming was a total computer nerd?"

Why You Crave Passion

Why do we spend so much of our energy trying to find that prince of a guy and build a cozy little nest for two? Sociobiologists say that our need for sex and our craving to bond with another person runs deep within our emotional DNA—a kind of glue that assures the survival of the human species. Apparently lust nudged our cavewomen sisters to forage for sex along with wild plants and, after they found a partner, to stay with him to raise a baby together.

We humans do not reproduce by budding or by sending out runners like strawberry plants or like characters in "Star Trek"—through telepathic communication. No, our sex drive is an inborn, primitive mechanism that sends out drumbeats signaling you to find a mate and make babies. There is, however, a loophole in Mother Nature's grand plan; even when you have no desire to "reproduce," you still desire love. And sex is still sex, whether you're doing it for intimacy, release, curiosity, or because you're just plain bored.

Other scientists scoff at the notion that love is an evolutionary impulse that exists only to hoodwink us into making babies. They claim love is a mythical illusion—a cultural invention, mostly a Western indulgence. Passion didn't rise from the swampy sea with us, they say, but rather evolved along with other cultural artifacts. Like wedding cake and table manners. Which means our culture teaches you how to be in love and how to express love, but love is not an inborn part of essential human nature. Lust, yes; love, no.

Dueling theories aside, it all comes down to this: passion connects you in a powerful and intimate way to someone else—in a way that nothing else can. Your craving for lust and romantic love and your need to bond passionately with one special guy are all stirred together in the same honey pot. Consult the *Kama Sutra*, the graphic sexual love manual of fifth-century India, and you'll find not only that our word *love* comes from the Sanskrit *lubh*, meaning "to desire," but that men and women have enthusiastically practiced the intertwining of sexual cravings with passionate love for a long, long time.

From the Roar of Lust to the Purr of Love

As unromantic as this sounds, to really grasp why you—like the rest of us—are so enchanted by and so desirous of love, you need to visit the brain, not the heart. Scientists are discovering that love activates a different part of the brain than do other strong emotional states, such as anxiety and fear. The brain waves generated by deep love's emotion travel pathways usually associated with addiction. Apparently the brain activity of love-sated people employs neural mechanisms similar to those that generate the euphoria induced by taking drugs like cocaine or by eating chocolate. You might as well face it: just as using cocaine or eating chocolate can be addictive, you can be addicted to sex and love.

When it comes to hooking you on sex, the brain is on overdrive. The more pleasurable sex is for you, the more sex you want, because your brain floods your nervous system with the urge to repeat it, repeat it, and repeat it and . . . don't stop now! Orgasm, the big O, is not only the release of sexual tension; the French say it is *le petit mort*—the little death. The afterglow of an orgasm can teeter on swooning, a sense of pleasure spun from the compelling creative energy of having experienced both the emotional submission of yourself to another person and the physical heart-stopping sensations of intimacy. When you have sex, you open up a part of you that is otherwise inaccessible to another person. And you experience him in a way that is otherwise inaccessible and that is unique to the two of you.

Sex is better for your body and your mental health than a trip to the gym for a workout. Sex exercises the muscles and the respiratory system. It heightens all of your senses—smell, touch, sight, hearing, and taste—and stimulates your blood to get flowing. And it triggers the brain circuitry for forming emotional ties between you and him. In one study, oxytocin—the chemical that generates our postsex calmness (or need to sleep)—increased three to five times its normal level during a man's climax and can soar even higher in a woman's orgasm.

Given the erotic thrills and the loving attachment you experience having sex, it makes sense that the despair and depression you feel after the end of a sexual affair is like withdrawal from any addiction. It gives a whole new meaning to the term *love junkie.*

Finding Your Way

Passion isn't just one emotion. It is a complicated emotional and physical journey from the place where you're aglow with sexual electricity to where you're "romantically falling in love" to being "in love" and then to the comfy feelings of becoming emotionally committed to each other.

The markers along the highway vary somewhat depending on who is doing the dividing, but love researchers say that the four phases of love's emotions are more or less the same: sexual attraction, infatuation, romantic love, and companionable love—add all of them up and you arrive at passionate love.

While there is some overlap between the phases, each has a discernibly distinct neurological and biochemical effect on you. Sexual attraction is closely aligned to the cravings of lust and is associated with infatuation—an exciting but fleeting phase—that can go away in a heartbeat. But if it doesn't fizzle, your emotions flow into the next phase, "romantic love."

Now you find yourself reacting to a series of related chemicals flooding your brain and body—dopamine, norepinephrine, and serotonin. And you begin to experience the rosy-hued euphoria of those amazing "head over heels" love emotions. In fact, people who have just fallen in love say they spend 85 percent of their waking hours thinking about their new lover. Since the neuron in this brain circuit communicates through the chemical messenger dopamine, researchers have cheerfully dubbed dopamine the "molecule of desire."

Although dopamine sets off the "can't think of anything but him" mind-set and puts you into a suspended state of romance, it is a phase with a short shelf life—usually a year, sometimes two. But don't let anyone knock it. Without experiencing the giddiness of romantic love you will never experience the emotions that are necessary to take you to a deeper level of passion and commitment.

As you move forward from the roller-coaster ride of sexual attraction through the maze of infatuation and then tiptoeing in a haze of romance—if you're lucky—a new combination of brain waves and sexual messengers infuses your system, those quieter, slower-burning "cuddle chemicals" of oxytocin and vasopressin that kick in an intimate bonding, nesting urge. You have now arrived at a place where you can stop and smell the roses and bask in the sunshine of being passionately, and at the same time comfortably, in love.

Can Lust Turn into Love and Vice Versa?

I'm often asked if being mostly sexually hot for each other can ever turn into a "being in love" relationship. Or, conversely, can a mostly "good friends" relationship get turned on its ear and become passionate?

Given that there are so many different factors at play in a mating scenario, it may be possible for a highly physical relationship to morph into a compatible lovey-dovey one and still stay hot. And it is possible that a sweet and loving companionable connection could erupt into a sexually lusty relationship.

Studies suggest that a switch in feelings is possible—but not probable—because the hormones connected with sexual desire might trigger the release of oxytocin, the chemical associated with love and romance. And there is some thinking that the chemistry of sexual desire can set off a chain reaction of romantic feelings. This means a casual sexual relationship could turn into a love relationship and, from the opposite side of the bed, a calm, companionable relationship could ignite into a sexual fire. But given most people's experiences, you can't count on either transformation. Usually, what it is is what it is. There are exceptions—like Andrea's story, which follows.

One thing is for sure: you can't fake how you feel. That *sizzle* of attraction mingled with the feelings of being in love with your partner is either there or not there.

Being Passionately in Love: Andrea's Story

Nothing brings together everything we've discussed about love and passion better than Andrea's story of how her relationship with her husband, Bill, evolved from lukewarm to friendly dating to a kissing connection to passionate.

"The best time of the day is getting in bed at night with Bill," Andrea says while sitting across from me, talking quietly in a cozy booth at a coffee shop. A few months ago, I was having lunch with a group of girlfriends talking about world peace and the men in our lives, mostly the latter, when Andrea told us something that intrigued me and that I couldn't get out of mind. She said, "I am so passionate about my husband." I asked her to tell me more.

"We have been married for thirteen years, and right now we are in a particularly 'close' period. We have always been in love, but right now we are on the same wavelength, a synchronicity. Bill and I met among a group of friends at a state fair. I was with two guys I was casually dating. But one got sick, and the other one had to give him a ride home. So Bill and I ended up on a kind of date. I thought he was nice but just a 'regular guy.' We went out the next week, and I liked him. I could tell he was a really nice person, honest with a lot of integrity. He was a good kisser, and I enjoyed kissing him, but I didn't see us as a romantic couple. He was much older than I was, and I just ruled him out as a potential serious partner. Besides, I wasn't interested in getting married for a long time (I was thinking I would wait until I was at least forty years old so I could be single for half of my life and married for the other half). We dated—about six months—and then for Valentine's Day he went all out. He made reservations at a cozy, intimate restaurant, arrived at my door wearing a tuxedo, holding a dozen long-stemmed red roses. Over dinner we were so engrossed in conversation the waiter told us he would buy us drinks at the bar if we would vacate the table. It began to dawn on me that he was 'the one.' It wasn't that lightning struck—not then—just a deep realization. Later we made wonderful love, and we gazed into each other's eyes, and I knew I loved him with all of my heart. I realize now that as a little girl I had dreamed that I wanted to love a man with all of my heart, without holding back, without reservation. Over the next three months we were constantly together, then one day it dawned on me, a feeling came over me— it was a 'Shazam!' moment—I knew I loved him madly and with all I have to give. Up to that moment, it hadn't felt completely right; now I knew it did. I know I thought to myself, This may really be it. This is what I want. But I still was hesitant about marriage until he said something that rang so true to me: 'Unless we get married and have the commitment of a married relationship, how will we realize the full potential of what we could be together?' Damn. He had me. He got me with logic. He was right. Things moved along, and we were formally engaged a few months later.

"I have such a strong passion for Bill because of who he is. He is an amazingly kind person. I love his spirit. I strongly feel so physically and emotionally connected to him, I sometimes feel vulnerable and emotionally overwhelmed. I love being with him; I can truly be myself. I don't have to self-censor. I still enjoy and need to be alone once in a while. But I like being with Bill more than anyone else."

I asked her, "What makes getting into bed with Bill every night the best part of the day?" Andrea sighed and said, "It is a special intimate time. We hold each other, enjoy being physically close, feel loving toward each other. It's not so much about sex—-it is about the depth of our feelings of being deeply connected."

What can we learn from Andrea's story? A passionate love partnership doesn't have to begin with both people getting hit by a lightning bolt at the same time. But the mysterious sexual energy that Andrea identifies as a "Shazam!" moment must eventually emerge to catch your heart on fire for you to be truly excited and content to be with him.

It Takes Two to Cha-Cha

You can enjoy the amazing things science can tell us about sex and love, and at the same time you can honor the mystery of being passionately in love, but you don't have to be blind to what is going on in your relationship. Has the sizzle clicked in for you but you aren't sure it has clicked in for him? If that is the case, you need to ask yourself what is really going on. For example, if he never initiates a "just wanted to hear your voice" phone call or checks in via phone or e-mail when away on a trip, if his face doesn't light up at the sight of you, if he coughs up saying "I love you" like a hair ball, if you are almost always the one making an extra effort to spend romantic and hanging-out time together, if having sex has become the prime reason to get together, if any mention of future plans for vacations or family holidays has him clutching the remote control and staring blankly at the television screen, it is what it is—likely a casual relationship but unlikely a passionate relationship with a future. Of course, the behaviors I just listed are limited in scope— clearly you need to do more detective work to come to any conclusion.

Nevertheless, it takes two to cha-cha—or, if you prefer, to tango. If you are spending too much time (you are the judge of that) wondering what he feels about you and whether you have a future as couple, it is only sensible to go to the source and ask him. If your feelings about the relationship (and each other) don't match, you are better off knowing what is going on—even if it forces you to reexamine how this relationship works for you. It is also worthwhile for you to know the truth even if it forces you to end the relationship.

A passionate love has to be mutual. Love can never be equal in intensity or in anything else between two people, but it has to be on the same level in the playing field. A one-sided or mostly one-sided love relationship will never be satisfying and is a one-way ticket to heartbreak.

When You Aren't Sure

You have seriously clicked with a man and believe there is a potential for this to develop into a deeply passionate and loving relationship. But somehow you aren't comfortable swimming in the deep end of this relationship pool with him. Pay attention to what may be causing you to feel that discomfort. Adjust your life jacket and tread water awhile. Don't jump out too soon; you may simply be reacting to being in a new situation or deep down are trying to avoid a rerun of the not-yet-forgotten heartbreaking past relationship. On the other hand, don't get all pruney by staying in too long. If, after three to four months of seeing each other on a consistent basis, you can't put your finger on what still seems off to you, listen to your inner gal. She is telling you that, whatever the reasons, he isn't for you.

Be kind, be gentle, don't string him along, and don't make up lame excuses about why you are ending the relationship. Either way, it will come back to haunt you. Don't be petty—it leaves lasting scars. Be generous; someday you may be in the position to form a lifelong friendship. Avoid the temptation to make a breakup promise that "we can still be friends." It is among the world's emptiest and most unwelcome of gestures.

The Four Factors of Passionate Love

In addition to the mysterious force of sexual attraction blended with being fascinated and enhanced by each other, there are four factors that play into two people falling passionately in love (more about each in later chapters).

- **The Ticktock Is Right.** You have to be at a time in your life where being in a partnership is more appealing than being alone.

- **Same Zip Code.** A lover has to be where you are. It
  sounds like the "duh" factor, but consider that it is easier
  to be in love with someone who is around than one who
  is geographically someplace else. Long-distance romances
  tend to fade away because absence doesn't necessarily
  make the heart grow fonder. For many of us, it turns into
  another cliché: "Out of sight, out of mind."
- **Common Ground.** Standing on some common ground—
  education, intelligence and ambition, religious values and
  political beliefs—is nice because you end up with a relationship without a lot of angst. But you don't need to be
  completely compatible; differences add a zing of intrigue,
  keeping the comfort zone from becoming a lackluster zone.
- **You Both Like What You See.** Although you may not
  be aware of it, there is a subtle, sometimes unconscious
  list of "perfect mate" characteristics that is etched in
  your brain (and he has his own "love map" etched in his
  brain). When you both find someone who has those characteristics, or close enough, you are likely to ring each
  other's romantic chimes and be drawn to each other.

Keep in mind that anyone can look good and be on his
or her best behavior during the courtship "getting to know
you" phase of a relationship. Take it slow and don't be anxious about and overly focused on the long-term potential of
the relationship. In many cases, as writer Charles Bukowski
observed, "Love is like the fog that sometimes blankets L.A.
in the morning. It softens everything and it burns off in a
couple hours."

After taking into consideration all of the above, know
that the most important factor in finding a passionate love
is opening your heart to whatever happens.

How Does a Passionate Love Fit into Your Life?

How do you feel about passionate love? Take a moment to respond to the questions in *My Passionate Love Story*—it is your own personal assessment of how you deal with love, sex, and relationships. There aren't any right or wrong answers. The questionnaire is designed to help you take off your emotional blinders to get a clearer look at why your emotions, expectations, and behaviors may be keeping you from having the relationship you need and desire.

My Passionate Love Story

- What's it like for you to be passionately in love? How would you describe your emotions?
- Have you ever had the experience of being in a sexually lukewarm but emotionally compatible relationship that grew in sexual passion over time? What changed it?
- When you are "falling in love," how can you tell if what you are feeling is real and not something else—such as boredom or an itchiness to fill a gap in your love life?
- Have you ever been wildly in love but then unexpectedly fallen out of love? What happened? Was it sudden? Or did it just slowly fade away? What were the dynamics?
- Have you ever experienced someone falling out of love with you? How did it end? What happened? Were you surprised, or did you feel the end was inevitable?
- Essentially, what do you think are the dynamics that move you from being sexually attracted to forming a close sexual and emotional bond?

- What qualities would your perfect romantic partner have? What is the most important and what is the least important to you?
- What are the most important romantic and sensual qualities you bring to a passionate relationship?

After you have finished reading the last chapter of this book, fill out the questionnaire again and compare your responses.

Embracing Passionate Love

After talking to countless numbers of people and collecting information as a researcher, I am sure that there isn't only one soul mate designated just for you and that all you have to do is to wait for destiny to work her magic. There are any number of someones out there you could be attracted to and fall passionately in love with.

Finding a partner means being in the same place where eligible men are—men who are straight and have never married or are divorced. Forget about those who say they are "separated" or those who are noodling around with esoteric notions of moving to Tibet and becoming a monk. To increase the odds of meeting a man you can love passionately, you need to meet all kinds of men (your type and not your type)—on the Internet, on a blind date, from a personal ad, from the files of a professional matchmaker, at a coffee shop—wherever people gather. (FYI, most single men are in Nevada and Alaska.)

Given the crunch of time in your life and the overabundance of personal "seeking long-term relationship" ads, speed dating, just-have-lunch dating services, and the online and offline professional matchmakers, it isn't surprising that you—like millions of the rest of us—can be confused and dazed about the best way to find a passionate relationship. It boils down to this: there isn't any one best strategy. Having friends fix you up with a blind date, gushing that he is "perfect" for you, can be a mixed blessing, but it is as scientific and effective as any other way. From my perspective, the strongest argument for using a matching service is that they offer you a chance to narrow down the playing field in a low-risk environment.

Near the sunset hour, we are all just hardy souls hoping to find "the one" or at least "a one" before it gets too cold and dark out there. In truth, the mate-selection code to match you up with a sensual and intimate loving partner has yet to be broken. As Helen, a market researcher, puts it: "You can make all the logical plans about how you will meet the person of your dreams you want to. But when two people meet and hit it off and then fall in love, it is just the luck of the draw."

For inspiration (OK, sometimes a guilty pleasure), read the "how we met" stories in the Sunday *New York Times* or your local paper's engagement and wedding announcement section. Some of the stories will make you, well, gag, but most tell wonderful heartfelt tales of finding someone against all odds. Then watch the DVD of *Love Actually*; it underscores the point that people find each other in the most unexpected places.

Given the sheer number of men out there, and if you are willing to give up on the myth that "all the good ones are taken," you are bound to find at least one man with whom you will share a passionate connection. Then go forth and write your own misty-eyed "I found my soul mate" story.

Have the Courage to Love

The key to authentically being loved and loving another person in return comes from understanding that intimacy takes guts as well as good intentions. You have to go out on an emotional limb to allow yourself to embrace the complexity, the magic, and the truths—sweet and bitter—of a passionate love. Don't put down roots until you have it. Because, as Rachel, a counselor at a university health center, told me, "Most of us believe we have been in love many different times in our lives, but when the real thing comes along, you realize that everything that came before was just so much practice."

2

Are You Ready for Passionate Love?

I was a mess. I had two interesting men in my life and couldn't seem to live with or without either one. One lived close by, the other a thousand miles away. Finally, each of them gave me an ultimatum: make a choice. Out of the blue, I received a terrific job offer that would take me many more miles away from both men. I wasn't all that unhappy with the job I had. And I owned my own townhouse with a great view of the mountains around Albuquerque. Did I move? Did I stay? Which man did I love more? Should I just say "What the hell?" and move in with the long-distance romance to test the deeper water? Could I bear to live without my loving hometown man? No question: I loved them both. So there I was, stuck in my ambivalence like a deer caught in the headlights.

My sounding board, my brother Phil, had heard the same old rumblings, the same old "Should I? Shouldn't I?" over and over, until he had heard enough. He wrote a nugget of advice for me on a piece of notepaper and handed it to me without comment. It said, "What are you willing to let go of to get what you want?" *Let go of?* The thought gave me pause. What was I holding on to for dear life—even if it was driving me crazy? In the midst of all my emotional upheaval, I came across Mary Oliver's wonderful words from her poem "The Summer Day." She seemed to be speaking directly to me, and she grabbed my full attention when she asked, "Tell me, what is it you plan to do with your one wild and precious life?" It became painfully clear: I wasn't only wasting time wallowing in my indecision; I was wasting my "one wild and precious life."

I began to take an inventory of my life from a different place than I had done before. I had to let go of my fears about making the wrong decision. I had to let go of my fear of being doomed to a life without a partner on a singles-only island. I had to start trusting myself to make a worthy decision. And if it didn't turn out to be all I hoped it would be, I would have to let go of my usual reaction when things went awry—reliving each downward turn of events by slapping myself on the wrist with a mental ruler and berating myself repeatedly for my stupidity.

I finally found the courage to fold up the relationship tent, took the job, moved my worldly goods, bought an enchanting condo that was like living in a tree house, and turned the page to a whole new life. The men? We went our separate ways. And when I think of the long-distance love, I smile and feel grateful I once had such a wonderful man in my life. When I think of the other man, I have a happy heart. After some time went by, we found each other again.

I taped that copy of Oliver's poem on my desk's bulletin board—next to my brother's note of advice—and look at both every day. I'm not claiming that two pieces of paper— a poem and a note—changed my life. They were (and still are) little reminder nudges to pull myself out of any self-dug ruts. What helped me take my life in my own hands were the conversations with friends and colleagues, the many wonderful men and women who talked with me about the meaning of those wise quotes and how we can apply that wisdom in our lives.

What Are You Willing to Let Go of to Have a Passionate Love That Is Real?

Making the most of your "one wild and precious life" begins with being scrupulously honest about what I call your "willingness" to be truthful about who you are. No one can do this for you because it lies only within yourself. Here is the key question: what are you willing to let go of to have a passionate love that is real and you can trust? This is as complicated a question as it sounds. It tests our mettle and has us walking a fault line between our desire to be sexually shaken to our roots and our protective impulse to be in a safe, sheltered love place. To free yourself so you can see yourself and others, you may have to confront long-held beliefs about love, sex, and relationships that have been shaping much of your behavior. Write down that question and put it where you can see it to give it its due while you are reading this book. Ask some friends the same question and really listen to their answers. Think through your answers again.

In this chapter, you'll focus on getting clearer about knowing what you want and how much priority and energy you realistically are able to give to an intimate relation-

ship. Then we will identify the choices we have about relationships, from marriage to being attached but not legally
attached to being unattached. We'll look at possible barriers—from the crunch of time to the lack of real motivation
to make changes—that have to be whittled down for you
to have the kind of passionate partnership you need and
want.

Wanting the Right Things

In the ABC television show "Desperate Housewives,"
Gabrielle (the beautiful ex-model with the trophy house and
a bottomless bank account played by Eva Longoria) offered
a poignant observation about her life: "I have everything
I wanted, but I wanted the wrong things." You don't have
to be desperate or even a housewife to discover you might
have been clueless about what you really want and need in
a relationship. Most of us go round and round, dating, not
dating, thinking about marriage, thinking about not being
married. The best way to get off that marry-go-round is to
take the time to know yourself before you put another person in a family picture.

What kind of a relationship do you want to be in? Do
you want to *be* married? Or *get* married? Are you smitten
with the idea of being a bride and experiencing a full-blown
"Queen for a Day" wedding with the white dress, brides-
maids, flower girl, and Dad walking you down the aisle? Or
do you believe that marriage is a unique and very personal
and private agreement between the two people involved and
the wedding isn't all that important?

Are you the kind of person who may be better off not married? Does having a copilot suit you? Or are you more suited to flying solo? Do you feel better plotting your own course? Do you have a strong desire to have a family? Do you picture yourself as half of a team of two, supporting each other in love, work, and family life? Or is it a romantic and loving partnership you seek, one without the strings attached to being married?

If your fairy godmother (or your personal goddess) agreed to grant you one wish about love, what would it be? A loving man to grow old with? An exciting wild and crazy guy to see the world with? Staying in an Italian villa clinging to a cliff over the Aegean Sea, where you can experience erotic sex with a different man every summer? Or . . . ? You get the idea.

The best way to respond to these questions is to curl up somewhere comfortable and conduct an interior debate with yourself. Hold forth intellectually and emotionally on the pluses and minuses from both sides of your inclinations at the same time. For instance, hear Ann's debate with herself regarding her personal tugs-of-war over the priority of dating over marriage: "Marriage would mean no more dating, and I'm worn out from dating fatigue. Marriage would mean Sunday mornings in bed and someone to spend the whole day with. Never having to worry about how sex fits into the relationship. But dating different men is exciting. I enjoy meeting a variety of men and experiencing new interests and hearing new opinions. And, in truth, I like the idea of having sex with someone new or someone that I like because I'm not obligated to him." Form your own debate issues and then start talking to yourself (out loud if you have a private place). Listen to yourself. What sounds to you like your honest bare naked self? What sounds more like the voices of other people telling you what they think you should want? Or what sounds like something you easily have said in the past but now has a tinny sound to your more mature ears? Even if you feel chagrined about how you really feel, put your feelings out there to examine them from all angles. Centuries ago, a very wise Chinese teacher named Lao Tzu said it this way: "He who knows others is wise; he who knows himself is enlightened." Become enlightened about the most important person in your life: you.

Out of that exercise may emerge an awareness of what you really want in terms of a loving, sensual relationship. Don't be surprised to discover that you are harboring conflicting desires, wanting togetherness and also wanting the freedom of being unattached. In fact, this conflict is often a powerful but unacknowledged source of tension in our ability to form or maintain a love relationship. Thomas Moore, the author of *Soul Mates*, makes an insightful observation about how the unresolved tension between those two claims on our heads and hearts affects us: "Many people seem to live the pain of togetherness and fantasize the joys of separateness or vice versa, they live a life of solitude and fill their heads with alluring images of intimacy." In other words, bouncing back and forth between a yearning to be connected and the lure of the sexy unknown means we never fully enjoy being in either state; we are always someplace thinking about being someplace else. Most of us never completely resolve those conflicting desires; they ebb from time to time and then appear to come out of nowhere. The best way to handle them is to acknowledge you are not immune to these inclinations and then be aware they are simply a part of being in an intimate relationship.

The Byways and Highways Leading to Love

There is no one road map to guide you down the best route to your relationship destination. No secret passages to finding love. People take any number of highways and byways to find a passionate partner, or to look for a little romance, or to keep things interesting in a longtime relationship. Let's take a moment here to step back so you can gain a perspective on the route you want to take, by checking out the ways other women are defining how love fits into their lives.

Being Single

Despite the billion-dollar marriage marketplace and the never-ending supply of enthused couples exchanging vows right in front of millions of people on TV, a sizable number of women aren't getting married. In fact, the most dramatic change in the relationship world as we have known it is the seismic shift in women's thinking about what it means to be single. Some women choose to be "attached" to a partner but not "married" to him or not be "attached" to any one partner.

The fact is that single women are not a monolithic group. Few single women have Manolo Blahniks or Prada in their closets. Few lead the legendary sex life of Samantha on television's "Sex and the City," and fewer still can relate to Lilly Rush on "Cold Case," who apparently has no sex life.

Women aren't single because they are too "picky" or "prickly" or because they have a gigantic "fear of commitment." Many single women are single because they haven't found the man they want to marry or they are exercising caution so they don't get trapped in living unhappily ever after.

There are, of course, many married couples who enjoy domestic tranquillity and seem to flourish in their married state. However, there is no shortage of examples of the dreary prospect of crummy marriages or of miserable married couples. But for many of us, it is the unhappily married couples that leave us with the deepest unforgettable impressions. Their constant bickering paints a grim picture of two sad and lonely people serving out a life sentence. In short, being single means not having to say you are sorry you made the wrong choice of a marriage partner. And at the same time, many women have told me they like being single because they enjoy the freedom of not being socially and legally bound to another person—especially if he has an ex-wife and children.

Being Married

Just as there are many different ways to be single, there are numerous ways you can be married. Look at the dazzling kinds of personally written and spoken marriage vows. Think about all of those on-the-beach nuptials or couples exchanging vows in hot-air balloons or while bungee jumping off a bridge. Yet the Census Bureau reports a new wrinkle in the fabric of the tapestry we call *marriage*: married couples' households are now a minority, making up about 49.7 percent of U.S. households, the smallest percentage in our marriage record books.

Tempting as it is to play "Taps" for marriage, though, it would be premature. It's not so much that most women and men won't ever marry; it's that they are getting married later. Taking in all adult age groups, about 32 percent of men and 24 percent of women have never married—a major increase since the 1970s. But among Americans between the ages of thirty-five and sixty-four, married couples still make up the majority of households. The numbers may shift to fewer married people in the post-thirty-five-year-old cohorts in the future, but marriage as we know it today, in some form or another, isn't a museum piece.

One reason women are stepping out of the conventional marriage box is that since the late 1970s more women are bringing home their own bacon and don't need to be taken care of. More of us are going to college, reaching parity in professional education, and setting our immediate sights on career building. And it's been a long time since a woman felt she had to be married to have sex.

For many women marriage simply isn't on the top of the "to do list" for now. It seems that women have many more options about whom to marry and when to marry than ever. Still, I sense a lingering whiff of nay-saying in the air about women choosing to delay marriage. You probably recall those famously off-the-mark social critics warning us that if a single, college-educated career woman is still blowing out the candles on her more-than-thirty-something birthday cake, she is doomed to hold the Old Maid card forever. The real facts are that marriage rates are actually increasing among college-educated women and men. For example,

among twenty-five- to thirty-year-old women, 88 percent
with advanced degrees have married, compared with 81
percent without college degrees. And once married, these
smart, successful women are no less likely to have children.
It turns out, according to Christine B. Whelan, author of
Why Smart Men Marry Smart Women, a majority of single
men who are in the top echelon of earnings (for their age
group) or are college graduates say they hope to marry a
woman who has a college education and who is successful
in her career. And along with success, these men say they
are seeking to marry a woman who is as "intelligent as they
are, or more intelligent."

It turns out that postponing marriage until you are over
twenty-five is a good idea; the risk of divorce is 24 percent
less than for those who get married younger. The good news
rolls on. Women who have graduated from college are less
likely to divorce when they do marry: only 16.5 percent
of their marriages dissolved compared with 38 percent in
which the wife had completed only high school.

Being a Romanic Roommate

Living with a man is not, for most of us, "living in sin" anymore; being a romantic roommate is getting close to a social
norm (admittedly, "living in sin" sounds like more fun).
There has been a steady increase in the number of people
who live together and choose to be a couple without being
married. They are, as the sociologists put it, "cohabiting."
In fact, that's about one-third of American households. At
one time living together was a way to test the waters of marriage before making a commitment or was, to some degree, a

"starter marriage." But not so much anymore. Marriage isn't always the intent of the couple. If they do marry, the living-together experience doesn't necessarily mean you will be happily married—the divorce rate is slightly higher than for couples who didn't live together before they got married.

The reason a couple's relationship seems to change after they marry is mostly that the contract of living together isn't the same as the marriage contract. For example, when you exchange wedding vows you promise to love and cherish each other in sickness and in health. But the unwritten vow for many living-together couples is, as a wag at one of my workshops put it, "To be together until living with you begins to suck."

Why Do Women Marry?

Since you don't have to marry anymore to live a socially approved life or to have sex without getting branded as a slut, why would you do it? Why marry? For most of us, women and men alike, becoming a parent isn't reason enough to tie a conjugal knot. I imagine that what makes you want to get married is simple—your desire to be married to one special person.

There is a glut of other hypotheses, such as the social exchange theory, which involves calculating the balance between what we put into a relationship and what we get out of it. Exchange theorist Gary S. Becker has either the most realistic or the most cynical view, depending on your perspective. He says that women and men get married "when the utility expected from marriage exceeds the utility expected from remaining single." He has a point. Each of us has our own personal criteria for measuring the pluses and minuses of singleness versus marriedness.

Although the romantic fairy-tale books on marriage have some tattered edges, close to 90 percent of adults eventually marry. And a good-size majority of married men and women report being "happily" married and say that a good marriage is "extremely important" to them. Moreover, for what it is worth, married couples report being more satisfied and feel more successful in their lives than their single peers.

Here is the true love story of marriage today: we get married later, we marry smarter, and we have more enduring partnerships than ever before. That's good news for women who weren't born yesterday, who are seeking a partnership of two equals, and who believe that marriage holds, for them, the greatest promise of happiness.

Create Your Own

Katharine Hepburn wasn't shy about discussing why she didn't have any desire to marry. She said, "I don't believe in marriage. It's bloody impractical to love, honor, and obey. If it weren't, you wouldn't have to sign a contract." Actually, marriage, despite the promises of togetherness and happiness, isn't something you do or get because you signed on a dotted line. You create the meaning of being married with another person. Any kind of committed relationship—whether one is conventionally married or not—is a personally created state of union. There are many ways to be in a relationship besides the Mr. and Mrs. (or Ms.) marriage or the mini-marriage living-together model.

You can invent or reinvent your own personal style of togetherness that fits your own personality and your partner's personality. You can design how you both want to live the shared part of your lives and how you can fulfill your unique destiny. Amy, a woman in her late thirties attending one of my seminars, described herself as "happily married." Amy then went on to share with the group that she found she needed to do the Virginia Woolf thing and have a room of own. So she rented a very modest apartment that is her private "turf," and whenever she feels the need to be in her own space—sometimes for a night or two, sometimes for longer—she stays there. One of the other women in the group told us she understood Amy's need for "space"—she had taken the guest bedroom and made it into "her room." Sondra added to our "married with a room of our own" stories by explaining that she travels with her friends or with a tour group for a few months every few years and by herself usually once a year, while her partner pursues his avocations and travels to his favorite place. In other words, you aren't stuck in old definitions of "being married." *You can custom-design your own form of togetherness.*

The Ties of Being Together

For many women, the alone-but-married or living-together model doesn't work. For example, Jill, a part-time community college teacher and writer, says she is bonded to her partner (and he to her) like "entangled underground tree roots." She explains, "We don't like being apart even for a single night. We both work out of the house a lot, and I love knowing he is in his office while I'm in my office down the hall. We enjoy being in the same space even if we don't see or talk to each other for hours. It is both sexy and comforting to be together this way. If he can't join me on a trip that would be for more than one night, I don't go, and vice versa. We've done the bit about being apart on trips in the past and were both too miserable."

Love Is Not All You Need

The relationship question for you may not be formed around the issues of singleness or marriage—your pressing issue might be time. Let me put it this way: do you have enough time in your life right now to devote to a passionate relationship? Not only to finding one, but having one? It is important to mull that one over. Because, to love, for example, in the context of Buddhism, is above all to be there: to open your mind and your heart to communicate fully with your partner. A passionate love partnership needs two people fully committed and engaged in their relationship. Again, ask yourself: is a passionate relationship actually something I can handle right now? One of the most important ingredients for intimate relations to jell is to spend, as the cliché goes, "quality time." This does not mean sending out multiple instant messages on some technical wonder to stay in touch.

Do you like the idea of being passionately in love more than the reality of being in a passionately intimate relationship? In your everyday life, is there room for a vibrant, loving partner? Is there space in your overly scheduled day to be an enthusiastic and loving partner? Are you the Queen of Multitasking, finding yourself thinking about other things no matter what you're doing? Are you too busy to eat breakfast and almost always too busy to return a friend's phone call? And when you get home in the evening, are you too tired even to think about communicating with another person? Some people are so burned out at the end of the day that they can't have a conversation of any consequence with anyone, much less the person they love. If all of the above describes you, you need to know that the Beatles had it wrong; love is not all you need.

To be a passionately loving partner means giving the one you love your full attention when you are together. To really be there, in that moment, you have to let go of your worldly cares and put the business of your life on hold. Thich Nhat Hanh, a Zen Buddhist monk, tells us that the most precious gift you can give to yourself and your beloved is making time to be with him, being present in the time you do spend together.

And sadly, that is hard to do. In your everyday life, your mind and your body are rarely together. Thich Nhat Hanh says, "Our body might be there, but our mind is somewhere else. Maybe you are lost in regrets about the past, maybe in worries about the future, or else you are preoccupied with your plans, with anger or with jealousy." To overcome those muddled mind-and-body "not really there" tendencies, he advises you to become mindful of your actions and say to your lover with the full sincerity of your intentions, "Dear one, I am here for you." For me, this means being willing to make enough room in your life to open the door to the possibility of letting an intimate partner enter, kick off his shoes, and stay awhile.

Setting Priorities to Avoid Wasting Time

To complicate this issue even further, if you can't give enough time to find or to enhance an intimate partnership, you'll actually be wasting time. If you can't give priority to being fully present in a relationship, you'll end up being frustrated, and so will a partner. That is what happened to Mari, who works for a Washington, DC, consulting firm. "I'm not seeing Anthony, the man I've dated for over three years, any longer," she tells me. "He said I am a workaholic. He wanted someone to do things with, take trips, enjoy movies, and enjoy fixing dinner together. And he claims I was never available. I know I do work long hours during the week and on a lot of weekends I am busy with my volunteer work. But we spoke on the phone every day, and we sent each other very sweet messages. When we were together, it was great. Out of nowhere he said that he saw so little of me it wasn't making any sense for him and he was going back on the dating market. I was shocked. I thought he understood how important my job and my community work are to me, and I thought he was fine with it." I wonder, if Anthony behaved as Mari did, how long it would have taken her to become unhappy with him and eventually end the relationship. No one wants to be someone's last or even next-to-last priority.

Given the level of dissatisfaction all around when there isn't "enough" time to spend with another person, you are better off waiting until you can juggle whatever needs juggling so you can devote time to the demands (even if positive and lovely) that are a part of being a couple. Any couple. If you're time-challenged, you're not going to be able to pull extra time out of a hat, but the following steps may point you in the right direction of making priorities.

Create two lists. In one, write down what you most value in your life—love, work, family, friends, recreation, and whatever else is important to you. Consider what you believe most enriches your life today. It isn't helpful to gaze into a crystal ball and envision what you hope your future will look like when your life is saner. Stay focused on the *here and now* and list what gives you the most satisfaction—prioritize up to five things—and makes your life feel meaningful. Don't list more than five because, as Ken, a counselor from Boise, Idaho, cautions: "Stop trying to do ten things in five minutes and adding more dos than anyone can get done in one lifetime. You end up never feeling satisfied about anything you are doing or having a sense of accomplishment for a job well done." Ken has a point: too many priorities produce a list of charming reach-for-the-sky ideas rather than down-to earth things that really matter to you.

Don't get waylaid by listing what your priorities *should* be—the kind that you believe might put you in the running for a Nobel Peace Prize in the Mother Teresa tradition for unselfish behavior. Write down what really are your personal priorities. If one of your priorities is to be a first-class skier and master the black diamond runs in Taos, write it down. You don't have to share your priorities with anyone else. This is your list, your life. You are the woman!

It may take you several days, off and on, to complete this part of the task. But don't make this task another one of your time-munching projects. At some point, cut it off—decide it is a good-enough list. What is important is to for you to separate the chaff from the wheat (whatever that is for you) to determine what you actually do value.

On the second list, jot down what changes you believe you can make to translate your paper priorities into your real-life priorities. Be tough here. Be realistic about what you can commit to act on in the immediate future. You may want to put down priorities for the distant future. And if you discover that a priority you listed isn't one you really want to devote any or much of your time and energy to, now or ever, cross it off the list. What is helpful about this exercise is that it can show you have a clearer picture of what is a priority and what isn't, especially given the limited amount of time to do everything you want to do. For instance, you might have listed "spending time with family" as a priority, but after you honestly consider what makes you feel fulfilled and happy and what you are willing to commit to spending considerable time and energy on, you would have to say "spending time with friends." You aren't a "bad daughter." It's not that devoting time to family isn't important to you, but it might not currently be one of your top five priorities. Keep in mind that this list isn't cast in stone and for now friends may be at center stage.

Everyone's priorities change from time to time; we change, our situations change, and so do our ideas about what makes our lives meaningful. Revisit your list from time to time to check out your progress and revise your priorities and your commitments to action. To paraphrase my guru, Yoda, "There is no try; there is only do."

Wrapped in the Cocoon of the Sisterhood?

Almost all of us agree that it is a challenge to make time in our lives for a passionate partner and a great relationship. Beyond the time constraints, something else can form a barrier between you and that man. It may be your membership in the sisterhood. The special kind of friendship that bonds women can be a subtle, or not so subtle, influence on why some women give up on, or put a low priority on, the quest to find a man to share their lives with. All too often women don't have the same level of connection with a man that they do with their close women friends. Why put much energy into finding a partner when your girlfriends cover you like a cozy quilted comforter, keeping the cold winds of the mating dance at bay? This comfort level you enjoy when you are with your women friends can smother much of your desire to spread your wings. You can be stuck in the status quo without feeling stuck.

A few years ago I lived in Atlanta, where my best friend also lived. I enjoyed her company so much I didn't feel an acute or even much of a need to have a man in my life. Whenever I did feel some urges to find a partner (yes, the sex thing), I found myself asking "Why do I need a man to spend time with when I get along so perfectly with Roxanne and I'm never bored?" We traveled well together and had great adventures. I wasn't lonely because I had a great playmate.

Eventually the ticking of the "getting older" clock got louder and louder and I made a conscious effort to give up some of my time with Roxanne to pay attention to being with a man I could love and enjoy. But it took a concentrated focus on the anticipated pleasures I knew a loving man held for me. Some women find a passionate relationship with another woman and share a special connection with their sexy female partners. I applaud them. But as a heterosexual woman I know my destiny is to share a double bed with a man to snuggle up to. Without question, women friends are special and are to be cherished over our lifetime. But they can't quite answer that heartfelt need we have for a man in our lives, in our beds. To have that man in our world, we have to leave the warmth of the fireplace and go out on dark and stormy nights, even at the risk of a bit of frostbite, to find a loving, passionate partner to share time with.

You don't have to let go of the joys of sisterhood to have a man in your life. Roxanne and I are planning for yet another great Carol and Roxie Adventure. What is important is to avoid retreating to high school behavior and withdrawing from your circle of friends when a man enters your life. That is sad, really. I'm talking about addition, not subtraction. Although you are pushed on the amount of time you have to spend with others, consider how fortunate you are to be able to increase the bounty of loving people in your life and thus reap the pleasures of wine and camaraderie over many future potluck dinners.

You and Newton's First Law of Motion

Given that you are reading this book, I am making a not-so-grand leap of faith that having a passionate partnership (if not now, then in the immediate future) or improving on the relationship you have is one of your top priorities. Moving beyond list making and considering actions you might consider taking, let's apply physicist Sir Isaac Newton's First Law of Motion (sometimes referred to as the *law of inertia*) to the way you approach finding or maintaining a loving and sexy relationship. Newton found that "an object at rest tends to stay at rest and an object in motion tends to stay in motion with the same speed and in the same direction unless acted upon by an unbalanced force." In English, objects keep on doing what they're doing. If at rest, they will continue to be at rest. If in motion, they will continue to be in motion. And the object will stay at rest or in motion as long as nothing happens to change that state. For example, if you hold a glass of water that is full to the rim, the water will just stay in the glass if you stay still. However, the water will spill over the glass if you move it too quickly or if you slowly move the glass and then stop suddenly or if you start to move the glass in one direction and then change the direction.

Are you wondering how Newton's theory applies to your life? For starters, if you are secretly waiting for the love of your life to show up on your doorstep with roses in one hand and a diamond ring in the other, you are guaranteed to grow cobwebs of disappointment. If you are not in a relationship and you don't make an attempt to move into a different status or change your direction, you—an object at rest—will continue to be stuck with the status quo. If you want to change your no-relationship status, you will have to put into motion some kind of "unbalanced force." An "unbalanced force" is anything that shakes up your status quo. It could be joining a hiking club, volunteering to work for a city project, clicking into an Internet dating site, signing on for new classes at the gym, going to a different coffee shop every day and checking out the customers, asking your friends to set up you up on a date, taking a good guy buddy out for a not-a-date evening at a party—whatever it takes to get you into motion and off square one. Or, as my mom would put it, "Get off your duff." The good news is that once you get in motion, chances are you will, as Newton's First Law of Motion states, "tend to stay in motion." And that means getting unstuck. Are you feeling anxious about making changes? Good. Anxiety about stepping out of the rut we have carved is a normal and common condition. The alternative is not really an option—staying stuck in a place you would rather not be stuck in.

Beyond the Magic Eight Ball

Although you may feel overwhelmed sometimes between the stress of work and the demands of everyday stuff, as I've said umpteen times, you are the only one who can determine how you will spend the fleeting days of your life. Does hearing the words "you are in charge of your own life" feel as exhausting to you as it does to me? The idea of being "in charge" makes me feel like that guy in Greek mythology destined to push the same boulder up the same hill and never reach the summit. It's tempting to go and shake up the Magic Eight Ball and peer into it for straight and simple answers: *Yes! It is certain!* And I admit that I often hope someone will appear holding a flashlight to guide me out of the dark and dense forest of Decisions! Options! Choices!

In truth, too many choices and decisions aren't really the problem. Quite bluntly, your capacity to make life choices is a glass half full or half empty depending on how you hold the glass to the light. And you are the better for accepting your freedom to make decisions about how to live your life as a glass very full.

A Vow to Loosen Your Heartstrings

Each of us—you and me—can change our lives, with or without a passionate partner in it, for the better by vowing every day to embrace our one and only precious life. Follow in the path of poet Dawna Markova, who vowed (in her book *I Will Not Die an Unlived Life: Reclaiming Purpose and Passion*), "I will not die an unlived life/ I will not live in fear/ Of falling or catching fire./I choose to inhabit my days,/ . . . To loosen my heart/ until it becomes a wing,/ a torch, a promise." Write it down; post it on your bathroom mirror.

Last, consider the gentle reminder I get from my friend Judith when she observes that I am obsessing over some undone task on my job and thus not paying attention to the bigger picture—for example, that I'm not getting any younger. She quietly reminds me, "Don't let the song die within you." In short, if you don't do what you need to do right now—right now—to have the kind of passionate love you really want to have, when will you?

3

Love Maps

Approaching Love with
Eyes Wide Open

I once loved a perfect man. We shared the same values about family and friends, politics, religion, our professional interests—and he was a smart, tall, handsome rascal to boot. He was "perfect." Everyone told me so. Still, despite all the signs that I had hit the jackpot of romance, I had this secret and uneasy feeling in the pit of my heart that I should be more thrilled about this stroke of good luck than I was. I kept telling myself that my inability to set our wedding date was due to an irrational "fear of commitment."

Then one day, picking him up from the airport, watching him walk toward me, I knew in a flash what the problem was: I wasn't all that sexually attracted to him. I loved him, but not passionately. I had literally talked myself into believing I had found the love of my life because I desperately wanted him to be that love. Even though I feared I would be alone forevermore, I somehow mustered up the courage to end the relationship. It would have been a disaster to marry a man I didn't have strong passionate feelings for—bad for me, bad for him. Breaking it off was one of the most painful things I've ever done. Even though I know it was the right decision, I still feel awful about it.

As a woman, you have cut your teeth on the fantasy of a dream lover, the "one." But it is a fantasy with a downside: you may not really see *him* at all, just a faux portrait of a man you have conjured up. It makes you susceptible to believing, ignoring signs to the contrary, that you are destined to be with a man who seems to fit your romantic ideal, or close enough.

In this chapter, you'll find clues to how to determine whether you are living in a love-smitten fantasy or becoming involved in a relationship that has the potential to be a significant, mutually loving, and sensual relationship. Admittedly, none of this is easy. Just as other emotions, such as anger or fear, can be stimulated or reproduced, any of us can conjure up the emotional state of being head-over-heels in love—at least for a while. To help you find your way through any residual rose-colored fog, you'll then find a list of the essential characteristics of healthy, sensual, and loving relationships.

Your Love Map Story

"I'm in love. I'm in love with a wonderful guy!" Have you ever just shouted it out? Let your emotions of love and desire burst forth in uncontrollable eruptions? Wept tears of joy? How spontaneous are those heart-rending "I'm in love!" outbursts? It depends.

You have been exposed to thousands of images of declarations of love in films and on television, from MTV to the soaps. Without any effort—or even much thought—you can call up many of the words, gestures, and postures of lovers. By clinging to the thinnest of threads, and by mimicking what you have seen lovers do and say, you can become a star in your own love story, playing the leading role of a woman madly in love to perfection.

Your love and sex data bank, drawn from the people you've met and the experiences you've had, is imprinted on your brain's circuitry by the time you celebrate sixteen candles on your birthday cake. Each of us carries in our mind this unique "love map," to borrow a term coined by medical sexologist John Money, a subliminal record of whatever you find enticing and exciting —or icky and off-putting— about love and sex. Including anything and everything, from the shape of a man's feet to the color of his eyes. The way your dad patted your mom on her fanny—or didn't. A policeman's uniform, the perfume of gardenias, the scent of a tobacco shop (some people love that smell). The first time you had sex and every time since. The first time you fell in love and the last time.

To help you get a clearer idea of how a love map might influence your love choices, I've listed a few things for you to consider:

- Do you tend to be attracted to the same physical type of man over and over? Why do you think that is? Could it be related to an early crush you had on someone—either in real life or a celebrity—or a close relationship with a special guy during your teen years?
- Do you tend to be attracted to a man whose looks and or demeanor remind you of a man you admire in your fam-

ily—not necessarily your dad (though it could be) but perhaps an uncle or a cousin? If so, how does that inclination, if any, affect your mate choices?

- Do you find yourself attracted to a certain man—either physically or emotionally—because you feel comfortable around him? For example, do you have the feeling that you must have met before because it feels so easy to be with him?

- On the other hand, do you tend to be sexually attracted to a man that is physically or emotionally *not* like you—say, someone from a different race or ethnic group? Would you say that you prefer "exotic" over "familiar"? What influences your interest in the exotic? Travel to foreign lands as a kid? Or enjoying reading exciting tales of the exotic in books, or a teacher's enthusiasm for travel, or listening to family or friends with "itchy feet" talking about their adventures?

- In the same light, do you tend to be attracted to men that have a different *cultural* background from yours? Would you say that "opposites attract" is the key to your becoming interested in a guy? How does that work for you?

- Similarly, do you find guys that come from the same background as you or that are "homegrown" on the boring side? Why do you think that is?

- Is there a couple you know personally (it can be but doesn't necessarily have to be your mom and dad or others in your family) or in films, books, or other media that serves as a "role model" for the relationship you want to have or do have? What it is about that relationship that appeals to you?

- Is there a couple in real life or in the media that has the kind of relationship you definitely do *not* want to have? What is it about that relationship that makes you feel negative about it?

Consider all of your responses to these questions. See any pattern there? Can you sort out what influences you—positively or negatively—to form a romantic relationship? Then consider what makes a relationship work or not work for you.

Understanding your love map can help you untangle the patterns of your romantic relationships. On the plus side, when you meet someone and you fit together like the parts of a jigsaw puzzle, you may have a seamless sensation of falling in love. For instance, when Arcadia met her husband, Rob, she said he felt "right" from the very start—"like I had known him all my life." She met him at a college dance and was "drawn into the deepest, brownest eyes I had ever seen." She laughs and says, "I actually got goose bumps. But he was with someone, and so was I, so we went our separate ways—at least for a while. Within a week we each broke up with the person we had been dating. Rob called me—I knew he would—and we have been together ever since. We love to do everything together—not in a smothering way, but we just enjoy each other's company more than either of us enjoy being with anyone else. We have ridden our motorcycles for weeks over long road trips and have a blast seeing the country together. It is hard to put our connection into words, but we believe we were just meant to be together."

When you feel a strong pull of destiny to be a couple, as did Arcadia and Rob, it may be due to having similar "love maps." There is also the possibility that you are playing out a love fantasy that will fade away before too long. To distinguish what is going on—if it is a true connection or a charismatic infatuation—means understanding what is causing you to be drawn to a certain man and him to you.

Understanding the Upside and the Downside of Love Maps

There is an upside to allowing yourself to become aware of the patterns of your love map—it can help lead you to a partner who feels right for you and a relationship that is soulfully satisfying. The downside to following that unconscious blueprint for a perfect mate is that you may be drawn to someone who resurrects an unresolved conflict you experienced at some point in your past. Or you may tend to fall head over heels in love with a man you couldn't possibly live with and end up being in a relationship that is in constant turmoil.

Keep in mind that not every man you fall in love with will be like the last one or the one before him, since each lover will have different combinations of the characteristics marked on your love map. Also, stay aware that your interest in a certain man may be an unconscious reflection of a past love, the one you still fantasize about "what if" it had not ended.

This much is certain: your love map contains powerful mental images of your ideal lover, the romantically perfect love affair, and what arouses you sexually, including the "right way "of making love.

The Addiction to Romantic Sugar

Every woman I have ever met has a love-mapped craving for True Romance—adoration from our Slayer of Dragons, the wooing with flowers, sweet kisses, and the heavy breathing of desire—which is a lot like craving chocolate. And once you acquire a taste for romantic sugar, it's hard to lose your sweet tooth.

Our addiction to sweets gets a boost from what I call the *Sleepless in Seattle* syndrome. The phrase comes from the classic "chick flick" about two people fated to be together even though their lives and geographical locations are a Mt. Everest-sized romantic challenge. After everything you can imagine creates barriers to keep them apart, they meet, on top of the Empire State Building no less. The film ends with thousands of women sobbing happily into their hankies (me too) because it gives us hope of reaching the summit of our True Romance quest. But outside the theater we are left clinging to the belief that our soul mate is, as Linda Ronstadt sings, "somewhere out there beneath the pale moonlight," and fate will bring us together.

The problem with True Romance is that it bogs you down in the belief that it is your destiny is to find that prince, marry that prince, and then decorate that castle. It sets you up to hold your breath until your dream lover shows up—an image of a man that few, if any, flesh-and-blood men can mirror. Not surprisingly, this ideal of a "Perfect Man" can cast a gray shadow over a committed relationship. Because expecting a man to live up to an idealized fantasy gets you stuck in a repeating pattern of disappointing loves. Putting a man on a pedestal means he is no longer real and there is no place for him to go but down.

Unfolding Your Love Map

There is good news: your love map is only imprinted on your mind, not chiseled in stone. By giving considerable thought to figuring out what has influenced you to think about love and sex in the way you do, you can become aware of the direction your love map is pointing you. A love map is especially effective when putting your critical thinking skills to work in concert with your heartfelt emotions. You can make the best of your love history by using it as a backdrop to your current emotions and expectations about finding and maintaining a passionate relationship.

Just as everything around you is constantly changing, your love map needs to be reviewed and revised. It is too easy to stay hung up on the notions of how to find a terrific man that was drilled into your head by your parents or by those romantic novels you scarfed up. And it makes no sense to cling to old love-smitten images and ideas about sex and relationships that you have outgrown and that blind you to what is actually going on in your life. You aren't obligated to be loyal to your past daydreams about a Colin Farrell kind of bad boy or a teddy-bear kind of guy like Hugh Grant. You are free to get a crush on whoever floats your boat now.

The Pressure of the "Too Fussy" Label

Have you ever talked yourself into believing that a certain man is the love of your life because the relationship landscape has been especially bleak for some time? Or tried to "make" yourself fall in love with a really nice guy because it seemed like the right thing to do? You aren't alone. Elisabeth, a travel consultant living in Washington, DC, says, "I finally stopped seeing Jake after an off-and-on relationship for nearly two years. He is such a great guy and would do anything for me. I know he loves me and would make a good husband and father. But as much as I respect him and love him, I was never 'in love' with him even though I wanted to be. I've had so many bad relationships with lying and cheating men, and here is this really good man offering me marriage and family, which I really want. And I just can't do it. I'm worried that I'm acting like a silly adolescent and being too fussy—and I'll never find anyone. And I really do want to have a family."

It is never easy to listen to your inner voices warning you that even though you have found a wonderful man, if you don't passionately love him, he isn't "the one." What dulls our senses is that too often we worry that we are just being silly twits or, like Elisabeth, we fear being told the mother of all accusations of why we can't settle down: we are "too fussy."

Look at it this way, as Bill Pullman, playing the role of the nice guy in—yes—*Sleepless in Seattle*, said when he graciously accepted Meg Ryan's dumping him, "Marriage is difficult enough without bringing low expectations into it."

He is so right. Marriage is supposed to last a lifetime, and to start it off with a relationship that you are "settling for" and one that doesn't elicit your excitement is a mistake. No matter what anyone else has to say about your choices in love, marriage, and relationships, keep in mind that they won't be walking around in your shoes.

Eyes Wide Open: The Plus Side

It is only natural, given the complexity of finding a passionate love, that most relationships don't pan out ("You have to kiss a lot of frogs before you find a prince" and so forth). We'll talk about how passion may cool down from time to time in a significant love relationship in a later chapter, but for now our focus is on dealing with the aftermath of a relationship that never got very far off the launching pad.

The plus side of discovering early on that your relationship is turning out to be nothing like you expected is that the letdown isn't all that difficult to deal with because you haven't had a chance to get too involved. You may feel cheated, but the ending of the relationships doesn't have to be a major deal. For instance, Rachel, a gradate student in biochemistry, recalls how she fell in love with a guy she thought was "special." But, she says, "He turned out to be more ordinary than I thought he was. More of a jock, less introspective, more like most guys I've met." Disappointed, yes; heartbroken, no.

What lingers after the reality hits you that he isn't the one for you can be a rejuvenated hope that, with what you know now, it will turn out better next time. You will also be a bit more aware of the need to curb any tendency you have to talk yourself into believing that a man is your "dream lover" before the evidence is in.

Being Real

To get a clearer picture of why, after a short honeymoon period, you have been so unhappy with some of the men you have met, make a list of your disappointments in relationships and your complaints about the men in those relationships. For instance, maybe a princely guy did come along but everything wasn't a 10 on the True Romance scale, so you decided he wasn't a prince to begin with? Ask yourself why your expectations were so far from your lover's actual behavior.

I'm not saying you shouldn't find a partner that is as good as you are—successful, attractive, friendly, adventurous, and a cut way above average. I'm not saying "settle." I'm saying, in two words, "get real."

What helps you wake up and smell the jasmine is to be—simply put—tuned in to the realistic possibilities, not lost in pie-in-the-sky daydreams. One great piece of advice about being "real" comes from a woman knowledgeable abut the mortgage loan business. She recommends that women approach dating like shopping for a house. First of all, shop in a neighborhood that is in your price range. This means not limiting your search to dream houses on Leonardo DiCaprio Lane or Ed Burns Drive—not many women can buy a home in that neighborhood. Despite our cultural belief in a classless society, celebrities tend to marry other celebrities and rich people almost always marry other rich people—although I grant you, there are some exceptions. We have all heard about the wealthy guy marrying a beautiful woman from a humble background—but these are labeled "Cinderella stories," and the key word here is *beautiful*.

Still, you don't need to restrict your search to bland but upscale developments or fixer-uppers in transition neighborhoods. Be choosy. Most of all, don't be afraid to end a relationship that isn't what you hoped it would be. Sometimes a house looks good during the walk-through, but once you inspect it more closely you see flaws that will require more effort to repair than you are up for. Sticking with the real estate metaphor: flip him. What is important is to get back out in the marketplace.

Keep an Open Mind

Before Sandra Bullock knew much about the man who became her husband, TV star Jesse James, she says she had tagged him as a "brutish bigot." She told an interviewer that she thought he was a chauvinist kind of guy. But then, as she learned more about him, she realized that she had made a totally false assumption. And he turns out to be her ideal partner.

The lesson here is that the next time you meet a man, even if he doesn't appear to meet much of your "ideal lover" standards, you should keep an open mind. There will never be a perfect partner that meets each and every one of your romantically idealized criteria, but a good number of men can light your dashboard up and signal the potential that they may be a passionate lover for you—if you let them.

Take Anne's relationship with a younger man. Anne is a magazine editor who tells me about her sixteen-year relationship with Curtis, who is thirteen years younger than she is. She says she was as surprised as a lot of other people when she began dating him. "If someone had said, 'OK, here is a prediction: You are going to meet a man who will be your partner for life. He is a woodcarver, thirteen years younger than you, and he is going to see your age and your grown-up kids as a bonus,' I would have said, 'Keep dreaming.' Falling in love caught us both by surprise, particularly me."

Granted, a spark of sexual attraction has to be there between you and a man for a relationship to catch on fire. But if it is there, even if he doesn't seem to fit the mold of the kind of man you are looking for, give him the chance to surprise you. Stay optimistic; it is a big market out there with a lot of different opportunities.

How Can You Know If It Is the Real Deal?

Listening to women and men talking about relationships, it has become obvious to me that many have seen only a dimly lit picture of what a passionate—a healthy, loving, and sensual—relationship looks like. Thus, here are what I consider to be the basics, along with some insights I've culled from different sources and experts, especially from my favorite psychologists, Sol Gordon, Eric Fromm, and Hara Estroff Marano. The list is by no means exhaustive; use it as a starting point. The items are not in any particular order; each item is important in its own way. What might be second on my list could be seventh on yours. That having been said,

here is my list of the most important characteristics that
need to be in a relationship for passion to flourish.

- Commitment to the relationship as one that is special,
  unique, and worth holding on to. It doesn't have to be
  an "until death do us part" marriage contract. It does
  have to be a mutually passionate, emotional commitment of loyalty, respect, and support for each other. If
  you don't believe that the relationship can grow into and
  sustain commitment and passion, you need to ask yourself, "What's the point?"
- You feel better about yourself when you are with him
  than when you are with most other people. He can't possibly "complete" you, but he can inspire you and appreciate your charm, your wit, your grit, and your intelligence.
  It would be good if your perfect green chile stew, your
  chewy chocolate chip cookies, and your uncanny ability to ski the black diamond runs were in there too. You
  need to be his champion as well.
- You need to like each other as much as you love each
  other. There is a difference. Trust me, the liking is priceless, and without it love doesn't stand a chance.
- The willingness and the ability to say honestly and tact-
  fully what you think, mean what you say, *and* hear what
  each other is saying. Some people call this "honest communication." For me that has become such a hackneyed
  phrase as to be practically useless. I prefer to keep it
  simple: can you talk to him about anything (OK, almost
  anything) and he to you? Do you listen to each other
  without censorship, correcting or editing language or
  ideas, or mentally racing ahead to jump in and make

your point of view known? Do you really care about what he has to say? Does he care about what you have to say? Is the sexual side 98 percent of the relationship and the sharing of concerns, wild and crazy ideas, sentimental memories , and pie-in-the sky dreams for the future a meager 2 percent? If that is OK with you and it is in line with his expectations, well, then fine. Enjoy the sex. But don't kid yourself that, as the song claims, you "got it all, just like Bogie and Bacall."

- You share a sense of humor. You both are willing to laugh at yourselves and the world out there. You don't have to chuckle at the same jokes; you just need to enjoy each other's take on life and love. It helps if once in a while you can react to a joke or a situation by elbowing each other in the ribs and share a naughty and clandestine laugh.

- A sense of adventure. A desire to keep the passion between you fresh and interesting by tackling new horizons—doing things that wake up the brain cells and bring a flush to your cheeks. Travel to exotic places, sure. Take cha-cha lessons even if you have two left feet. Stretching together in a new yoga class counts too.

- Equality. A conscious sense that you are equals—not the same, but equal in all things, especially in respect for each other's personality and intelligence. This includes a shared responsibility for managing finances and going about the daily grind of domestic chores along with equal opportunities for gratifying careers and creative ventures.

- Buying into the same big-ticket items: morality and values. You don't have to agree about everything, but your

relationship will avoid teetering constant ly on the edge
of disagreement and arguments if you are both on the
same altruistic and practical wavelength about how you
view the world. Consider how *deeply* you feel about the
some of the big-ticket topics I list here and to what degree
you would be comfortable "agreeing to disagree." The
big-ticket topics include politics—both global and local—
religion (being an active member of a specific faith or
church), including the role of religion in government,
environmental concerns, waging war and peace, and *Roe
v. Wade.* The greatest deal breaker arises when one partner wants children and the other definitely does not. You
can't negotiate a compromise because there isn't one.

- Developing a catalog of shared experiences. Things you
  do together that define your partnership, from taking
  walks to painting the whole house to celebrating special
  rituals and traditions that you both enjoy.
- Last, but one that is actually before or right after commitment: you have to be sensually tuned in to each other.
  You have to want to kiss him, smell him, lick him, and
  crave sex with him. Not a romanticized version of "making love" but rather the erotic skin-to-skin, eye-to-eye sex
  with him. Sweet loving, of course, counts, and it has its
  place in our sexual repertoire, but nothing connects the
  two of you to each other like the sweaty, heart- racing
  expressions of mutually shared sexual passion.

Putting the Pieces Together

The following exercise is deceptively simple. Yet many of
the people who have done it at my workshops report that
it has been very helpful to them in determining their rela-

tionship priorities, and in many cases it opened the door to conversations with the man in their life they wouldn't have had. A woman from Tucson told me she keeps the results on a bulletin board and reads them over from time to time to see what has changed for her. Many times she finds her priorities have changed without her having been aware of the transformation at the time it happened.

Here is the question: what qualities, emotions, or characteristics about a passionate love are important to you? What do you hope to have in a relationship? You'll need eight pieces of paper. Tear a large sheet of paper into eight pieces: fold the paper over once, then again, then again, and carefully tear (or cut) along the folds—or use small note cards.

1. On each of the pieces (or cards), write a quality or an emotion that you believe is important in an intimate relationship. Now start arranging and rearranging the individual pieces of paper in order of your personal priorities. Think about the priorities you selected over a few days. Revisit them and make changes by rearranging them.

2. If you are in a relationship now, put a check mark on each priority that is being met in your relationship. You should have marked at least half of them with a check mark. If you have checked off only a few pieces of paper, you may want to reflect on what seems to be lacking and, most important, how you feel about the situation. If this is a new relationship, ask yourself if it appears to be worth investing more time and effort to see where it takes you.

If you currently are in a relationship, invite him to do the same exercise. After he is finished, share your results with him and discuss what priorities you share or don't share. This simple exercise can produce some valuable insights into yourself, him, and the two of you as love partners.

Your Passion "Carpe Diem"

Wishing on a star for an attractive man you have just met to be "the one" isn't enough to make that dream come true. Don't set up the expectation that this initial attraction will lead to a magical romance worthy of a novel. This could be the beginning of a beautiful friendship or a sexy, enduring love relationship. Or not. Relax, give it some air to breathe, and see where it leads you. Keep in mind that most sexy interactions have a short shelf life, and that is OK. Experiencing a flirty, jittery, rosy-glowing feeling of being passionately and sexually alive is a treat all its own, for however long it lasts.

In the final analysis, you are more likely to find what you want and need in a lover when you stop looking for True Romance and instead view the search for a partner more like a spontaneous road trip to uncharted territory. Just head out and see where the wind takes you. Make it a trip with a destination of discovery. As one mystic put it, "The journey is the destination."

Is Love Hot
Enough for You?

4

The Sizzle of Attraction

It happens in a nanosecond—without any warning—we feel a heart-stopping lightning bolt (as the French call it, *le coup de foudre*) in the most familiar of places, in the most unlikely of places, and at the least expected times, usually with a complete stranger. What happens when that bolt of lightning strikes?

From Dee, a Washington, D.C., lawyer: "I was almost at the exit door to the post office, and he was coming in the entrance, and I swear my heart missed a beat. Just like that, he dropped a pile of packages, and I helped him pick them up. He was the sweetest man, kept telling me 'Thank you, thank you.' I can't explain it, but I knew he was 'the one.' I gave him my card and told him to give me a call sometime when he wasn't playing postman. He called that afternoon, and we had dinner that night. I still laugh at what he told me about how he felt when we met. He said he was 'instantly, just like Baloo, the lovesick bear in the movie *The Jungle Book*, solid gone.' And that's why, he claims, he dropped those packages. We've been together ever since."

News anchor Brian Williams says that love happened while he was making other plans. He was walking through the halls of his office and turned the corner to almost run into a woman holding a stack of tapes. "I'd always read about the dynamic of lightning bolts and little cupids fluttering around, and I've never really believed this happened. But I'm afraid I couldn't stop staring at her." After his broadcast, he went into a friend's office and announced, "I think I met her." And indeed he had; June and Brian have been married for close to twenty years.

Callie, a woman at one of my seminars in Oklahoma City, tells me how she met her partner, Jessie. "I was in San Francisco attending a meeting and went out on a no-date dinner with a girlfriend and two of her guy friends I hadn't met before. One of them turned out to be Jessie. I thought he was cute, and we had a nice click of being able to talk abut a lot of different things. The other guy invited the three of us to fly with him on his private plane to Monterey for dinner the next day. During that plane ride I felt an out-of-the-blue "electric spark" between us. I know it sounds totally slutty—but Jessie and I began to make out big time. It wasn't planned; it just happened one deep kiss at a time. I have never felt such sexual attraction, such physical craving, for a man, ever. He came to see me a month later, and we spent the whole four days in bed. I moved out to San Francisco six months later. From that first kiss, the sexual passion between us was immediate. Now, after eight years, it is as much over the top and incredible as it was then. I never get enough of him. There are weekends we still spend most of the time in bed having sex, talking, having sex."

Being jolted by that spark—that sizzle of sexual attraction—is something you can dream about and light a few candles in the hope it hits you soon. But when it does, it may still surprise you. You can't completely comprehend the overwhelming power it possesses to set into motion your passionate emotions until you experience it. But you can pay attention to the clues about what triggers that sizzle and your intense sexual interest in one specific man and, if you are lucky, his interest in you.

In this chapter you can uncover those clues by tapping into a rich bounty of research from evolutionary psychology, cultural anthropology, sociology, and scientists who are breaking new ground every day—the DNA sleuths, the sexologists, and the biochemists. Keep in mind that while there is agreement among most researchers about the underlying triggers of sexual attraction, there isn't universal agreement about what takes you into a deeper level of passionate desire. No one "truth" or theory has captured the market or has unlocked all the mysterious secrets hidden within your passionate emotions.

Nevertheless, you can benefit from learning about what makes you tick sexually from each of the different "truths" and from men and women's stories of falling in lust and finding love. Keep an open mind as we travel though this tunnel of the "science of attraction" and you'll gain a deeper understanding of what sets off those drumbeats within your heart and, better yet, how to interpret the messages they are sending.

What Creates That Sizzle of Attraction?

Why do John's dimples drive you crazy while Steven's leave you cold? Why do you tremble all over from the vibrations of being turned on to one man but not myriad others? Why is one particular man attracted to you while another man isn't?

Before we venture out to find the answers to those questions, you might want to use the following quiz to take inventory of your expectations and opinions about sexual attraction and desire. To that end, I've listed a few questions to help you clarify your thinking about what attracts you to a man and ways to handle what you are feeling.

The Lightning Bolt Quiz

- What turns you on? How do you feel when you are sexually attracted to a man? How do you experience those sparks—that sizzle—of attraction?
- How do you know that what you are feeling is the hot breath of sexual attraction and not something else, such as boredom or an itchiness to fill a gap in your love life?
- What turns you off? How do you know you are *not* sexually attracted to a man? What are the clues to what you are feeling?
- What do men find sexy about you? Don't do a modesty cop-out and say "I don't know." Give yourself permission to tell the truth. It is important for you to honestly acknowledge your sexually appealing strong points.
- How do you deal with the situation when a man is clearly attracted to you but you don't feel the same way? What do you say? What do you do?
- How do you pursue it or "take it to the next level" when you are sexually attracted to a potential lover?
- In your experience, can a new relationship, one that is sexually lukewarm but interesting, change and grow

in sexual passion over time? Or do you think the sizzle must be there initially or it is a no-go?

Now the short-answer section. Love, it is said, has the power to hypnotize us, fog up our glasses, and render us temporarily blind. So, what is your response to this provocative question, posed by John, a thirty-something executive from Florida: "If love is blind, why do women spend so much money on sexy lingerie?" (See my answer at the end of this chapter.)

Consider revisiting your responses as you continue reading this book. You may see things more clearly through newly polished lenses.

Listen to the Beat of Your Heart

Love at first sight is actually more like lust at first glance. What makes you sexually attracted to him may be something fleeting—a smile, the sound of his laugh, the way his shirt fits over his chest, the color of his eyes—that is deeply embedded in your passionate DNA. To learn more about what makes your heart turn cartwheels, you need to check out the major theories. For example, some anthropologists claim the way we feel and behave about sex lies mostly in culture. Sociobiologists contend it is mostly in our genes. Evolutionary psychologists argue that although both of those theories have merit, we also have to trace our behavior to the evolution of the mind. Just as we have evolved physically, we have evolved mentally. And when it comes to the sexual mating dance—he takes that step, she takes this step—evolutionary psychologists tell us that our seductive behavior is shaped by a powerful and cunning Stone Age psychology that woos us into making babies. What is important to know is that men and women with all kinds of physical and personality traits make up the meat and potatoes in the sexual stew that has been on a slow boil for millions of years—and sexual chemistry is the spice that makes the stew so tasty.

Take your pick of what motivates you "to mate"—whatever makes the most sense to you. But there is one nondebatable point: women have never been passive participants in the mate-hunting game. We have been engaged in a sophisticated game of shrewd strategizing and savvy negotiating that leaves its stamp on how we deal with men today.

The Most Important Factors That Kick In That Sizzle of Sexual Attraction

What pushes you in the direction of being sexually attracted to a specific lover is closely linked to many nuances of your sexually fine-tuned DNA in combination with those messages about romance that our culture has been whispering in your ear since you were born. To help you sort it all out, here, in no particular order, is a list of different factors that researchers swear are the most influential.

The Arrows in Cupid's Quiver

What moves you forward from being sexually attracted to him to being sexually aroused by him? Singer Vonda Shepard (from the "Ally McBeal" TV show) nailed it perfectly when she sang the Sixties hit "The Shoop Shoop Song (It's in His Kiss)." I love that song because it instantly reminds me that it is a kiss that leads us into the wildest territory of our erotic impulses.

You have a desire to kiss him because—are you ready for this?—you've been shot with an arrow from Cupid's quiver, one that was dipped into a cache of chemicals that blindly bathes your brain with an invisible and seductive elixir of hormones, endorphins, pheromones, and phenylethylamine. That rush of "love" chemicals stimulates your giddy sense of sexual attraction and heightens your sex drive—all because you are in close proximity to a person you find desirable. It is a sensation that is comparable to the effect of an amphetamine because you experience the euphoric emotions of optimism, giddiness, and contentment. For lack of a better description, it mimics what you have learned to recognize as the sensations of "falling in love."

The Scents of Love

Any number of stimuli—his looks, the way he kisses, a full moon, or music—can arouse you, but the bedrock of seduction is found in the natural odors of your man and in the essences of scents as varied as red roses, cactus flowers, citrus, gardenia-perfumed candles, vanilla fresheners, and musk after-shave lotions like that sure-fire lady killer, Polo.

To be blunt: your nose leads you down the primrose path to passion or pushes you into the nearest escape route. The source of sexual attraction is literally in your nose. It turns out that there is a recently discovered sixth sense, a tiny organ in the nasal cavity that responds to chemicals known as *pheromones*—nearly a dozen different odorless chemicals produced by human skin. These pheromones play a role in basic human emotions such as fear, hunger, and, yes, sex. Scientists have long suspected that people, like insects and some mammals, cast a mating "influence" on each other via sexual scents transported by those pheromones.

Working with a team of scientists, David Berliner, an anatomist, found that several of the human pheromones appear to be sensed only by males or only by females. He believes this suggests that they serve as "signals" between men and women. It could work for us in the same way as it does, say, for moths. In that case, pheromones act as chemical attractants that lure members of the opposite sex, sometimes from miles away.

A SNIFF OF YOUR SWEETIE. If you have ever secretly taken a whiff of a piece of clothing your lover has worn, you have a lot of company—I bet almost every woman you know has done the same thing. And think of those movie scenes where our heroine-in-love takes her lover's shirt and rubs it on her check and then takes a deep sniff of it. Reading about "sniffing" scenarios in cold print can make you feel a little silly and a lot self-conscious, but take heart; there is something within you that compels you to act that way.

Take, for example, you and a man's T-shirt. Professor Martha McClintock conducted a provocative study about a woman's mate-seeking detector and a man's odor, especially a T-shirt worn by a man on two consecutive days. The T-shirts, free of all scents except the man's, were placed in boxes where they could be smelled but not seen. Unmarried women were asked to sniff the boxes and choose the box they would prefer "if they had to smell it all the time." The women were attracted to the smell of a man who possessed genetically similar traits—but not *too* similar—to their own gene pool. The study's findings reflect our best evolutionary instincts.

Apparently there is a finely tuned "genetic code" in a man's scent that a woman can use to avoid mating too close to home. Therefore, we seek a mate with genetically based immunity to disease different from ours. This difference helps assure a wider range of desirable gene combinations to strengthen disease resistance to help a baby thrive in a dangerous world. McClintock explains, "Mating with someone too similar might lead to inbreeding."

Not only do you as a woman have a superior sense of smell, but you also have keener interest in your partner's smell than he does. You need to be choosier than he is about whom to have sex with and "mate" with because you have to consider the cost of a nine-month-long "morning after" and the years of motherhood ahead.

There is a caveat here: researchers have found that women taking oral contraceptives can be dangerously misled in their choice of a partner. It seems that women on the pill report being attracted to the smells of men with quite similar genetic profiles. The pill tends to reverse natural preferences, and a woman may be attracted to a man she wouldn't normally pick as a mate if she wasn't taking it. (One theory here is that because a woman is vulnerable during pregnancy and childbirth, she seeks the protection of close kin when in that condition.) Just in case, if you are using the pill, you should consider trying an alternative kind of birth control before committing to your partner—to test the air, so to speak.

WHEN LOVE AND SCENTS DON'T MIX. We have no control over what is pleasing or repulsive to us. Some people smell exciting and wonderful to us, and others don't. Simply put, left to its own devices, body scent plays a silent role in whom we find attractive. Each of us has a unique "smell print," and what is provocative and alluring about one man's odor to you is an offensive turnoff to another woman.

PHEROMONES AS APHRODISIACS. Clearly you are sexually influenced by chemical sexual signals that you can't see or hear. But the main effect of these sexual pheromones isn't torrid passion; rather, they fuel you with a general feeling of well-being. They help you feel more confident and easygoing, which may put you in a socially upbeat mood, hopefully up for a little romance. Based on those notions of pheromones as feel-good signals, a company called Erox (too coy) is designing fragrances that affect the person wearing the fragrance, not the opposite sex. That is, Erox plans to use the pheromones sensed by females in its products designed for women and put its male-sensed pheromones into products for males. Because the wearer will feel "sexier," he or she is more likely to attract the opposite sex—or so Erox hopes.

Erox stops short of calling its bottled pheromones *aphrodisiacs* because there is little evidence that either a man or a woman can attract a mate by pheromones alone. Apparently an irresistible fragrance hasn't been invented yet. So beware of those perfumes with pheromone-based additives that are billed as aphrodisiacs—they can't offer any kind of guarantee you will be able to attract the man you want to attract.

The best way to embrace the role of fragrance in your sex life is to pick a scent that makes you feel sexy and desirable, one that doesn't clash with your skin's natural aroma, and not use so much that you cover up the best thing going for you—the way you and you alone smell.

After the Sizzle: What Draws You to a Certain Man as a Potential Partner?

Given that a spark of sexual attraction—with at least some degree of heat—has ignited, what happens next? What takes you to the next level of being drawn to him and interested in pursuing a relationship? I've culled through the many studies about what might draw you to a certain type of man, or to a certain man, to help you better understand what sparks your sexual attraction desires. Following you'll find a synopsis of the research, ranging from what causes you to take a second look to how men and women "rate" each other to what goes into your choosing a cad or a dad.

Agreeing About What's Sexy

A man sitting across from you catches your eye. If you both like what you see, it may be because you share a frame of reference for what is sexy and appealing.

While movie stars and celebrities are widely admired for the beautiful and handsome creatures they are, most of us—both men and women—rate faces near the average as the most attractive. (This is true in societies as diverse as those of Chile and Great Britain.) Beauty aside, this is because average faces tend to be more symmetrical than nonaverage, and it is that symmetry that appeals to most of us—it is a sign of healthy and non-crazy-making genes.

It may sound a bit creepy, but studies say that if your boyfriend has the same eye or hair color as your Dad, it might not be a coincidence. We tend to choose partners who look like their opposite-sex parent. And the way you bonded to your parents can also influence the type of sexual attraction and attachment you form as an adult.

How He Rates

Unless you just woke up from a hundred-year sleep, you won't be surprised to hear that men and women play the sex game differently and tend to choose a partner based on different criteria. For example, men claim they are turned on by a woman's breasts, buttocks, and eyes, in that order. Women rank eyes first, buttocks second, with lips and "the bulge" tied for third place.

From a mind-soul perspective, not surprisingly, men and women also differ on how they rate the importance of "personality" characteristics in a potential partner. Women say they admire and are turned on by "intelligence, kindness, and confidence." Men say they appreciate those qualities, but they generally rank them less highly than women do. Men tend to rate honesty and a sense of humor higher than most women do.

Women, as a group, are somewhat less concerned about a man's handsomeness than we are about whether he gives out clues that he will be willing to invest time and resources in a relationship. Overall, women tend to be more concerned than men are with a prospective mate's ambition, status, and what kind of resources he has to offer. This "Breadwinner Fast Track" legacy is changing but is still so powerful that women size up a man's finances or Fortune 500 CEO potential even when they don't have to. Women who are on a fast economic track themselves tend to be interested in men with fatter checkbooks who have financial prospects that are equal to or greater than their own.

Psychologist David Buss surveyed more than ten thousand people in thirty-seven cultures on six continents. He claims that if our criteria for an eligible mate (men valuing a woman's physical attributes; women dreaming of a moneyed slayer of dragons) were culturally driven, you should expect to find at least one society somewhere out there where women's and men's ideas of an ideal mate were reversed. But he didn't, which tells us that men and women's different turn-ons are a fundamental part of human psychology.

Men and the WHR

Apparently many men judge a woman' s figure as appealing based not so much on whether she is slim or chubby but by the ratio of her waist to her hips (scientists refer to this as the waist-to-hip ratio, or WHR), with the ideal proportion being hips roughly a third larger than the waist. Researchers believe men are attracted to this ideal ratio because it reflects a hormonal balance that results in women's preferentially storing fat on their hips as opposed to their waist, a condition that correlates with caveman notions of higher fertility and resistance to disease. Although it is disputed, some scientists say that while our culture is obsessed with slimness in women, and the winning Miss America has become 30 percent thinner over the past several decades, in most instances the contestants' waist-to-hip ratio has remained close to the old ideal.

Here is a strange twist: while men desire highly attractive and youthful women with the ideal WHR when they are playing the field, they say they will actually settle for something less than that ideal in a woman they desire to be in a long-term relationship with. Not very flattering news for wives and live-in girlfriends, but there it is.

The Hands of a Man

In addition to all of the preceding information on how you are consciously or unconsciously attracted to a potential lover, there is one more subject to consider. Check out his hands, especially his fingers.

The website Chemistry.com claims it can match your personality traits to a "type" based on the level of your neurochemicals and hormones. For example, visit the website's "scientifically based" assessment quiz and you'll find an image of a hand followed by a question: "Which of the following images most closely resembles your right hand?" You get to choose among these answers: index finger slightly longer than ring finger; index finger about the same length as ring finger; index finger slightly shorter than ring finger.

Helen Fisher, the site's well-known anthropologist, designed the test and says that if your ring finger is longer than your index finger, you are likely to be a director type (rational, analytical, logical, narcissistic, and competitive—testosterone alert here). If your index finger is longer or the same size as your ring finger, you are likely to be more of an estrogen-infused personality, such as a builder (calm, stable, constructive, creative type) or a negotiator (creative, humane, insightful, agreeable, flexible).

It seems that the ratio of finger lengths, especially the lengths of the second and fourth fingers in a particular way, is determined by one's exposure to estrogen and testosterone in the womb. Thus, check out his fingers and you may get a clue to his inner testosterone or estrogen.

A recent study more or less tackled the same topic of using a person's finger lengths as an indicator of levels of testosterone and estrogen. According to the English University of Bath's study of men in academia, men teaching hard-science subjects such as mathematics and physics tend to have index fingers slightly shorter than or as long as their ring fingers, indicating that they have testosterone levels above or equal to their estrogen levels. Men who teach in social science subjects, such as education and psychology, have a more equal index–to–ring finger ratio, which could indicate a slightly lower testosterone-to-estrogen ratio.

The finger ratio link to our personality type is still less science and mostly speculation, but it is an interesting speculation. From another angle, it is often said that the size of a man's feet, or the shape of his hand, or the length of his fingers indicates the size and shape of his penis. Undeniably, *that* is an interesting observation, but further research is needed to prove or disprove it. Any volunteers for that study?

The Allure of a Dad Versus a Cad

When you are mostly interested in finding a short-term partner, your preference for a manly kind of man increases substantially. However, if you are looking for a long-term relationship, you will be especially interested in a man who likes children. And according to a recent study, you are very likely to be able to tell which men would be a good bet for a long-term relationship just by looking at their faces. You are also likely to be able to figure out by their facial characteristic which men have the highest testosterone levels, which rates them as the most masculine and, according to the women in the study, perfect for a fling. "Women make very good use of any information they can get from a man's face," says Dario Maestripieri, coauthor of the study, "and depending upon what they want and where they are in their lives, they use this information differently." In her study, a group of men aged eighteen to thirty-three had their saliva tested to determine testosterone levels and then were shown ten pairs of photographs or silhouettes, each with an attractive female or male adult and an infant. The men were photographed as they rated their preference. Photographs of the men's faces were then shown to twenty-nine women aged eighteen to twenty. The women were asked to rate men on four qualities—"likes children," "masculine," "physically attractive," and "kind"—and asked to rate how attractive they found each man for short-term and long-term romance. The women did well in rating the men on the qualities "likes children," and "kindness." The men rated by the women as more "physically attractive" and "masculine" did turn out to generally have higher testosterone levels than the other men.

What also affects your perception of a potential partner depends on the available pool of men and whether you perceive those guys as looking for a committed relationship or a "one-night stand." Anthropologist Elizabeth Cashdan of the University of Utah asked hundreds of men and women whether they thought the members of their "pool" of potential mates were considered trustworthy, honest, and capable of commitment. She also asked them what kinds of tactics they used to attract mates. She discovered that when people thought their potential mates weren't honest, they pursued short-term dating tactics. For example, if a woman considered her pool of potential partners to be populated by "cads" (lacking in honesty and ability "to commit"), she reported that she usually dressed more provocatively and was more open to casual sex. If, on the other hand, she felt the pool was mostly "dads"—that is, committed and nurturing men—she spotlighted her qualities of fidelity and loyalty and dressed less provocatively. To attract a woman, men who called themselves "cads" said that they tended to emphasize their sexuality, and men who called themselves "dads" said they relied more on advertising their desire for long-term commitment.

On one hand, these studies do confirm the theories that you are programmed to be attracted to a man who would be a great dad. On the other, I think it should give us all confidence that we can recognize a man who isn't such great Daddy material but one we can enjoy as a delightful dessert.

Taking the Time to Look Twice

If you find yourself gazing into someone's eyes from across the room and are ambivalent about what you see, don't turn away too soon. Researcher Dr. Shinsuke Shimojo of the California Institute of Technology in Pasadena advises us to "stare just a little longer." It could tip the scales in his favor.

According to Shimojo, whether you are initially interested in a man is partly determined by the amount of time you spend sizing him up. When the participants in her study increased the amount of time they spent looking at one face over another, the one that got more "face time" won out in a "likability" rating. "Gaze is a critical component for humans," says Dr. Shimojo, "and by playing gaze catch-ball we can increase friendliness, attractiveness, and intimacy." In the real world, you have to be careful about whom you are staring at and for how long. Staring at someone on a New York City subway may set off a stampede of frightened fellow passengers heading for the next car. Still, the idea that it pays to take a second and longer look at a stranger who has some potential to interest you makes a lot of sense.

Love "Is" What It "Is"

Before you assign either the glory or the disappointment of your love life to your inherited cave sister's or your mom and dad's DNA, take a long deep breath and remember that you are susceptible to any number of sexual nuances and influences. There isn't any one essential "reality" that explains why you are sexually attracted to one man and not another. Or what propels you into—as songwriters from Cole Porter to Alicia Keys soulfully describe—"falling in love." I admit I'm partial to science writer Hannah Block's point of view. "Love," she says, "is a commingling of body and soul, reality and imagination, poetry and phenylethylamine."

Here is Naomi's unique story of a head-over-heels attraction and what happened next.

"I was delivering material for a newsletter to his house, rang the doorbell, and he opened the door. He was a tall, handsome man with beautiful 'silver fox' hair and a soft-spoken southern manner. I was blown away. I can still recall how I felt at that very moment—like someone singing a Tony Bennett ballad—love at first sight. I was in a hurry and couldn't come in, so he leaned against the doorjamb and we chatted a few minutes. I couldn't tell you a thing we talked about—I only remember his voice, his persona, and the effect he had on me. Over the next couple of years, I would see him occasionally at large parties for some political cause or another, and he was friendly. I had the worst secret crush on him, but I was married and he was married. End of story? Not quite. My life changed—got a divorce and finished a college degree. We met again at a huge campaign party—and I'd be a liar if said I was sorry to hear he had gotten divorced. We went out for a postparty drink and spent hours talking in an old dark bar with plushy red leather seats. And the rest, as they say, is history. I've told my friends countless times that I know I am lucky because not only do Patrick's looks totally captivate me but, as a plus, he is good on the 'inside'—he is a really kind, thoughtful, and loving man."

While science can give you helpful information about what draws you to another person, it isn't the be-all and end-all. For example, when it comes to the rating game, it isn't really useful to rank a person's specific characteristic as your ultimate turn-on, because no single feature stands alone. Butts are attached to a body with a heart and a head with eyes and so forth. A man's physical characteristics are only a part of him. You have to know a man through both the ups and downs of life to determine whether he has intelligence, is kind, and is confident and, if so, what he is confident about.

You need to know him over some length of time to determine whether the personality traits you are observing are real or mostly a sham. Take the research about women and men's physical and personality preferences into consideration and then assess what you think sounds reasonable in terms of what may or may not apply personally to you.

He's Your Man, Not Their Man

To find that passionate man you deserve, continue to shift your gaze away from conventional wisdom's narrow focus on a companionable life partner. Take a wider, deeper look at what kind of relationship makes *you* feel sexually and emotionally fulfilled. He may not fit the mold of past lovers; in fact he could be a sea of change for you. Don't get sidetracked by what others think you *should* have in a relationship.

The man in your life you are attracted to may not win a popularity contest among your friends and colleagues. But he needs to win a vote of confidence from only a majority of one: you. Sure, it is reassuring when others you care about like and approve of him, but they aren't in the relationship; you are.

Having said that, however, if you are hearing a lot more negative press about his character and very little positive feedback from really close friends, consider pumping the brakes. Allow yourself to slow down and see how you feel about him over the next couple of months. Even if it is hard to do given the power of our lust-love emotions, do it.

Play Him or Trade Him

You are attracted to him—just not in a major sexual sizzling way—but you enjoy his company and can easily say he is a "great boyfriend." You are on the cusp of a decision here. If a passionately sensual and intimate partnership is what you crave, you need to play him or trade him.

In the first option, you can put energy into stoking the fire. There is no guarantee that anything you do will turn up the heat, but if this is a worthwhile relationship, it may well be worth the effort. You can—alone or together—seek the advice of a sex therapist to increase your abilities to communicate and trust each other as you pursue a mutually satisfying sexual relationship. And/or you can attend workshops and retreats on enhancing the sexual side of a healthy relationship. Or pick up some tips from the many good "how to make sex hotter" books, videos and DVDs you will find in abundance in bookstores and on the Internet.

Hopefully your efforts will pay off: a spark will ignite the embers of a smoldering sensual chemistry. Be aware, however, that it is very challenging to make it so. If the sexual chemistry doesn't kick in by six months or so, you may want to consider the trade option.

In the long run, denying or ignoring our yearning for a passionate, sensual love doesn't work. Faking our feelings or pretending that it doesn't matter is disastrous for the relationship in every way. Eventually the lack of sensual pleasure erodes the quality of the partnership and leads to frustration and disappointment, even despair, and often to divorce.

Be Aware of Your Lust-Love Emotions

There are many invisible forces triggering what could be a *sizzle* moment for you when you meet an attractive man. Be aware of what is making you feel the heat of those sexual sparks. Before you get carried away, take an inventory of what you are really feeling and what is actually happening:

Is what you are feeling an earth-quaking encounter measuring a 6 on the Lust-Love Richter Scale, or is it really mostly a tremor? Is it possible that your interest in him might be connected to feeling just a wee bit desperate to make a connection at this moment of your life? Or is it that he appears to have the trappings of a "good catch" (however you define it)? Or is it about your genuine attraction to him? Take a moment and ask yourself why this specific man is so appealing, so sexy.

Next, try to determine if the sexual attraction appears to be mutual and worth pursuing before you start planning for a future weekend together. Pay attention to signals you may be getting from him that he is interested you. You already know what to look for, so I've only listed a few "clues" here to jiggle your memory:

- Does he lean over to get close to you, laugh at anything mildly funny you say, ask you about yourself, look you in the eye (not over your shoulder, checking out the room)?

- Does he offer information about himself in a casually friendly way without offering TMI (too much information) about the sad details of his last broken relationship, references to his crummy childhood, or his impressive array of boy toys, and the like?
- Does offer you a card or a phone number and ask you to call him, or does he directly he ask to see you again?

For whatever the reason, if you begin to surmise that you are much more interested in him than he is about you, don't take it personally. You can't control whom you are attracted to and who is attracted to you. Just politely move on—you have a lot more frogs to kiss.

And Now for the Puppy Paradox

Five attractive men show an interest you. Four of them are very attentive, but the fifth walks away. Chances are you will be most interested in the fifth guy. Psychologists give complex reasons for this "interest in the disinterested party" phenomenon, involving the ego, a love-starved childhood, and so forth. But I think it isn't that complicated. Within all of us is a desire to run and the love of the chase (think of the kids' game of tag). But it is not possible to chase and run after someone who is standing still. The only person you can chase is the one who is running away from you.

When it comes to attracting a lover, a proven way is to adapt the same strategy you use to attract a puppy. You attract the puppy by getting its full attention and then dashing off while looking over your shoulder, smiling, and tossing out friendly little challenges: "Come get me!" The puppy will happily chase after you. If, however, you run *toward* the puppy, chances are that the puppy will run away and try to hide. What interests the puppy is the chase and the potential of catching you, not having you catch him.

So it is with men.

Love Is Not Blind

My answer to John's question: "If love is blind, why do women spend gazillions on sexy lingerie?" Because we like the way it makes us feel and look and we like the way our partner responds to how we look and feel. Scientific or not, it is no secret that sexy lingerie is a mutual turn-on—which is priceless. So, allow yourself to enjoy wearing and showing off that sexy lingerie that makes you feel like a sensual woman. And on that topic, we move on to the next chapter, "Revealing Your Inner Vixen."

5

Revealing Your Inner Vixen

"Seeking shortsighted woman with an enormous appetite for sex." We were listening to the radio in the car and heard that ad from a reading of personal ads found in an English newspaper. Something clicked, and I remembered hearing Nancy Friday's presentation at the American Association of Sexuality Educators, Counselors, and Therapists. In the Q and A following her talk about men and sex, she was asked, "When it comes to sex, in a nutshell, what do men want from women the most?" Nancy tossed her head back and without hesitation clearly pronounced: "For her to be hot, hot, hot!" Women applauded. Men gave her a standing ovation.

Are you harboring any *good girls don't crave hot sex* ghosts that inhibit you from enjoying being the erotically hot woman that is your birthright? Or, as the poster I saw outside of an erotic film festival in San Francisco put it: *"Santine Caloris Tibi et Est"* (Is Love Hot Enough for You)? You can put any lingering qualms to rest by tapping into the heart and soul of your own passionate and unique sexuality.

In this chapter, you'll learn ways to create your own sexual style that feels both comfortable and exciting to you. Among other things, we'll talk about what men find sexy and desirable about a woman, the keys to valuing your female sexuality, and how to apply eight fundamental truths about sex and seduction to your love life.

What Makes a Man Drawn to a Woman?

Beauty alone doesn't make his heart skip a beat. A great body is an enviable plus, but it isn't a sure thing. A sparkling personality does help. But it takes something else for a man to notice and appreciate you. Bill, an environmental advocate, single, and in his early forties, responds to my question about what attracts him to a woman, specifically, what makes a woman desirable and sexy: "What makes a woman sexy is that she believes she is sexy. And she has a way about her that makes you feel sexy too. She pays attention to you but isn't playing with you by coming on to you or playing the role of Miss Congeniality by agreeing with every word you utter. Actually, I like a woman with a little bit of an acid tongue—a slightly cynical side to her nature—one who is passionate about something in life other than relationships and who can hold her own in a no-holds-barred political discussion."

John, who is listening, couldn't resist joining our conversation. "I personally love to see a woman walk into a room and own it without being arrogant or pushy. I'm attracted to a woman who has an easygoing way about herself. Especially if she is a flirty woman, one with a great voice. A major turn-on for me is a woman who isn't afraid to laugh out loud. I love hearing a woman really let it all hang out."

Almost all men tell researchers that they, like Bill and John, are drawn to a woman who oozes confidence about who she is—a strong, smart, sensual woman. A woman who clearly loves being a woman and owns her own personal slice of the world has men eating out of her hand.

The first step to becoming more like one of those sexy and desirable women men adore is to turn up the volume on the inner voice that's encouraging you to reveal your confident, saucy, sassy self.

Sex Appreciation 101

First of all, none of us has sex in a vacuum. You bring every positive mind-blowing or negative never-had-an-orgasm-with-him experience, every anxious, ambivalent feeling you have ever had about sex, everything you have ever learned—both facts and myths about sex—to each and every sexual encounter.

Both men and women say that they want to have great sex. Yet something doesn't add up. It is a conundrum: we say we crave great sex—passionate sex—yet most of us say we only rarely experience sexual bliss. What gets in our way is that we are not really convinced we can handle passionate sex and thus we don't allow ourselves the pleasure of experiencing it. Tasha, in her mid-thirties, tells me she is "leery" of having out-of-this-world intimate sex because she "fears losing control, of not being able to handle the intensity." She says, "If I give in to my real sexual nature, I worry that sex could take over my life."

It's true that passionate sex is a force of all its own. It combines the sweetest of romantic emotions with an aching acute desire to express and receive sweaty, gritty lust. Connecting with this level of intensity means you can be emotionally overwhelmed and at the same time fear that he could reject you at your most vulnerable moment. But the intensity of passionate lovemaking won't turn you into a love slave, unless you want to be a love slave. In its essence, passionate sex dissolves boundaries, bonding you in a primal form of intimacy. It's not about gadgets, magic blue pills, or Victoria's Secret. It's about having the courage to let yourself be open to the amazing pleasure your body can give to you and your partner.

The Green Light

A woman's willingness to accept herself as an erotic, passionate woman is the conduit to the sensual pleasure of sexual desire. As a woman, you have a brain that is organized in such a way that you have readier access (than men do) to the emotional content of what you are experiencing. To let yourself "have sex" you need to experience a psychological go-ahead, a green light in the mind. For if sex is to be had, you have to say yes. You have to be convinced that there is no danger in this intimacy, that there will not be any repercussions such as his thinking less of you or no longer being interested in you postsex. Not surprisingly, a woman is less likely to experience orgasm during a one-night stand than she is in the context of a stable, long-term relationship. Still holding back and not allowing yourself to experience satisfying sex in a relationship you feel safe and secure in—casual or committed—is living in a world of fewer colors.

Finding the Diamonds Between Your Legs

What happens when we cross our threshold of sexual comfort? Follow me to the Society for the Scientific Study of Sexuality's meeting in Redondo Beach, California. I was walking around the exhibits and looked up to see a banner over a booth: "Live Like You Have Diamonds Between Your Legs, *Love, Badmimi*." On the table were piles of colorful satin and lacy pillows shaped like artist Judy Chicago's female vulva plates from *The Dinner Party*. Under folds of a satiny mons veneris, a large, shiny, clear jewel depicted the clitoris. A woman at the booth gave me a postcard with Badmimi's motto written over a graphic of a buxom naked woman with sparkly diamonds peeking out from her pubic hair. Their credo: "Thou shalt love your Vagina deeply and with reverence. It is the doorway to heaven. It is the place where souls come from heaven to earth, whether you choose to give birth to a soul or an idea, rejoice in the sacred essence of being a woman." My initial reaction? I was, I'm chagrined to admit, conflicted. On the outside I gave it a go to look "with it," but on the inside, while I was happy to see women's sexuality out there, I was blushing.

If I, as a well-established sex researcher and president of the Society for the Scientific Study of Sexuality's Western Region (and a self-proclaimed seasoned woman who wasn't born yesterday), was having trouble sorting out my feelings, how did other women feel? I cozied up to other women near the exhibit and quietly asked them about their response to the display. Most said they were happy to see a celebration of female sexuality, but for whatever the reason, they felt a little embarrassed. Only one out of eight women I spoke to didn't exhibit a single tinge of embarrassment. Without hesitating she bought three pillows to give to her girlfriends and one for herself. My hero.

My conflicting feelings gave me pause to think once again how difficult it is to rid ourselves of old and now unwelcome lessons that we learned at mother's knee about keeping our female sexual "parts" under wraps. Women in my seminars say that while they camouflage it pretty well, they still struggle to overcome the negative messages heard growing up—that women have an unsightly, off-smelling, unappealing place, vaguely located "down there."

The best way to turn around any negative residual feelings about your sexual physical self is to define yourself on your own terms. Envision yourself as an erotically sensual woman who, like Badmimi, has valuable and desirable diamonds between your legs—and then watch men worship at your feet.

Eight Truths About Women and Sex

Many women say that they learned how to enjoy lovemaking by educating themselves and through their varied love and sexual experiences. Others say their lovers were their most important erotic guide. While women's sexual education varies, there is a common thread weaving together their stories: accepting yourself—plum shaped, pear shaped or apple shaped—is the keystone to becoming the sensual lover you want to be. Once you understand the following truths about women and sex, you will be more able to stop acting from someone else's emotional script about what is sexy and write your own stories about the kind of lovemaking that feels right to you.

1. Sex Is Less About What You Do and More About What You Feel

There are any numbers of ways to heighten your capacity to enjoy more intense, more intimate sex. What counts is what turns you on—what makes you feel excited abut sex—and what brings you pleasure. If you are turned on and willing to embrace full-out sexual pleasure, your partner will absorb your enthusiasm and respond with even more enthusiasm. Sharon, a forty-something lawyer, says she and her partner have a terrific amount of heat between them but had gotten into a routine that made sex humdrum. "We had a frank discussion about wanting to have sex that held some surprises for each of us. One thing we do is take turns being the aggressive partner and the passive partner. I enjoy feeling a range of responses from being dominated with a little rough sex, to slow and easy and sensual lovemaking. It's fun to take on a role that is different from my usual personal style."

Every woman has particular erogenous zones, which are especially sensitive to different kinds of touch, and there are as many different combinations of erogenous zones as there are women. What feels sexy to one person is a major turnoff for another. What makes for great sex is discovering what feels sexy to you and tuning in to your partner's desires.

Compromise and trade-offs (I'll do this, if you'll do that) as a way to spark your sex life may seem like a fair way to go, but in practice you are left as a couple with a limited repertoire that guarantees tedium, not to mention resentment when one partner feels pressured to play a game he or she isn't comfortable playing.

2. To Have a Passionate Lover, You Have to Be a Passionate Lover

Fortunately, many women today have gone beyond thinking about sex as a guilty pleasure. Women think about over-the-top lusty sex and are just as interested as men in having hot, hot sex. In fact, women report wanting to have more sex than they are currently having and want to have a more satisfying sex life.

But in bed, you may hold back because you worry that he (especially if this is a new relationship) could be put off by your "dirty girl" proclivity. Because, despite being a woman who loves sex, you still carry around in the pockets of your psyche an old-fashioned handkerchief—one that reminds you that only "sluts" would do "that." Or if you are in a committed relationship, you may hold back out of concern that you might make your partner feel inadequate—falling short of being the sexy stud muffin you fell in love with. Or you may feel uncomfortable about wanting to kick it up a notch because you've learned from somewhere that sex is supposed to be mostly a mutually loving and caring experience.

The best way to face down any lingering worries and fears is to ask yourself, "What is the worst thing that could happen if I let out my sexy inner vixen? More of just-not-really-satisfying sex? Your partner is put off or is stunned and exhausted, even shell-shocked?"

Now consider the best thing that could happen: you have shared your honest, fun-loving dancing queen and your sensitive, sensual self with your partner, and he loves it. Together you are discovering what feels good to you and what feels good to him.

So stop worrying about embarrassing yourself or looking foolish while trying on a new or revised sexual persona. What counts is to let yourself have fun in bed, to sometimes be very nice and sometimes be very naughty. *(Because there are so many really good books that offer specific, step-by-step instructions on how to have the best sex of your life, I'm not going into the particulars here. Check the "Resources" section in the back of the book.)*

3. You Must Put a Bow on Your Package

Clearly, buttoned-down, predictable sex can be boring, the antithesis of passionate sex. Ironically, many of our most admirable societal beliefs about intimate partnerships, the values of equality and sensitivity can, in the bedroom, result in very dull sex. Among other things, sexual passion thrives on erotic power plays, anticipation, fantasies, mystery, and the games of being seduced and seducing.

Men get sexually turned on by what they see. And it is so easy to give a man a sexy thrill—one that holds a hint of a naughty side of you. Outside of the bedroom, particularly when you doing everyday kinds of things together or out at a movie or restaurant, no matter what you are wearing (even those old plaid cutoffs), let him know you are wearing something hot and sexy underneath. Let him take a peek. Only a peek. Go about what you are doing and occasionally flash him. When the time is right, have fun letting him unwrap the outer level to get to the gift-you. Men love the idea that a woman will wear sexy lingerie to please and turn them on. Most of all, they love to untie your bows.

Seduction is that sensual pleasure that heightens the tension pulling you away from your partner and the tantalizing tensions drawing you closer. Seduction doesn't have be a major production number—sometimes just a tease of naughtiness, a glimpse of desire is enough to get his (and your) heart pulsating

4. Passionate Sex Is Safe Sex

It's not especially sexy to talk about contraception, but how can you experience great sex if you let yourself be vulnerable to an unintended pregnancy or one or more of the nasty STDs that are out there everywhere? Years ago, in my book *Swept Away*, I wrote about how dismaying and perplexing it was to hear so many women say they took risks because they got swept away in a moment of passion. Others said they didn't want the man to think of them as too easy (read: slutty) by being prepared to have sex—the birth control being the evidence. Or he was reluctant to use protection and they didn't want to press the issue because they didn't want to turn him off and cut off the potential of a relationship. These ill-advised tactics to appear virginlike—considering the risks involved beyond his (a guy who is certain to be a nonvirgin) opinion of her—aren't worth it.

While women are better contracepters today than they were then, far too many smart, accomplished women still admit to having sex without protection. For example, 27 percent of women in a recent survey say they rarely or never use a condom with a new guy, and I bet they have the same excuses as did the *Swept Away* women.

You've heard it since high school, and if I've said it once, I've said it a thousand times: buy, carry, and insist that he use protection, until you are in a sexually exclusive relationship and both of you have been tested for STDs and HIV. And of course you have to use a method of contraception to avoid getting pregnant when you don't want to get pregnant.

No one enjoys having to use protection and contraception, but it is better than any alternative. There are different ways to incorporate contraception, especially condoms, into your lovemaking, so no excuses. And it is good to know that women who feel protected during sex have more orgasms than women who are worried abut pregnancy or STDs.

5. A Woman's Sexual Desire Surfs on High and Low Tides

Your hormones, stress, worries over money, jobs, children, or relationship woes, and happiness all affect your libido. Sometimes you feel hot; sometimes you don't. How a woman will experience a lack of sexual desire isn't predictable. For some women it begins as a slow drain on their sex life; for others it is roller-coaster ride of ups and downs.

The changing landscape of your sexual desire isn't a problem per se. I know women who, when they aren't in a committed relationship, say they have gone for months (some a couple of years) without feeling desperately horny. Being indifferent or being turned off to sex becomes a problem if it affects your sense of well-being. If you are in a committed relationship, it is as certain as the sun coming up every day that your lack of desire will cause tension and put a serous strain on your relationship.

If your sex temperature seems to have become set mostly on cool to cold, there are any numbers of ways you can overcome that iffy libido. First of all, check in with a sex therapist or health clinician to rule out any medical or other problems. That issue aside, the following lists some of the ways that may be helpful.

- **Try natural aphrodisiacs to boost your sexual desire.** Some scientists claim that the roots and shoots of passion are ginseng and ginkgo. Ginkgo isn't on a typical list of aphrodisiacs, particularly if you are feeling the sexual side effects of antidepressants. But it takes a while to show any benefit. Ginseng is considered to be a body-strengthening tonic, and studies are finding that it increases the body's production of nitric oxide, a compound essential for sexual response. Others, not as familiar, are those herbs that include muira puama, known as the "potency wood" in the Amazon because it heightens a woman's libido and increases the likelihood of orgasm. Consume coffee and chocolate. Women coffee drinkers are more likely than other women to call themselves sexually active. Chocolate contains phenylethylamine, a natural antidepressant and stimulant that, as you may know, has been tagged the "molecule of love" because it imitates the brain chemistry of attraction and sets off a sexual spark.

- **Maybe try pink Viagra?** There are pluses and minuses of pharmaceutical remedies designed to stoke the fire of sexual desires, such as "Pink Viagra" in the form of testosterone therapy such as creams, patches, and pills. Mostly the jury is still out on whether it is very effective. So, check with your health care clinician and test it out to see if works for you—it might.

- **Getting over feeling frumpy.** When you sense there is a distinct possibility that you will be having sex with a man for the first time, does anxiety abut exposing your body come up on your mental computer screen? Betty, a woman in late thirties, describes her first-time-with-a-man sex jitters: "When a new relationship begins to look in the direction of the bedroom, I become painfully aware that once again I will have to face some awful decisions. How much of my body should I reveal? I have small boobs and a 'fanny pack' of fat right below my tummy. Should I insist that the lights be off? Should I wear a sexy piece of lingerie? Should I wear a longish T-shirt and casually remark it seems chilly in here? Or is it too obvious I'm covering up? Should I show off some of my considerable sexual skills to divert his attention from my not-so-lithe-and-trim body? Or would that make me look slutty and/or desperate? Sometimes I have decided not to have sex because I'm not up for the physical exposure."

If you, like Betty, believe that your body is not desirable, your sexual libido and sexual confidence will take the greatest hit. As writer Sally Kempton put it: "It's impossible to defeat an enemy who has an outpost in your head."

Researcher Pat Koch and her colleagues found that the more a woman perceived herself as attractive, the more likely it was that she experienced sexual desire, orgasm, and enjoyment or frequency of sex. Conversely, they discovered that when a woman feels "frumpy"—unattractive and fat—she is more likely to feel less sexual desire and report having less sex. The most important way to get in touch with your sexuality is to turn a deaf ear to any negative, self-defeating voices telling you that you are "frumpy." And then to allow yourself to be comfortable in your own skin.

6. Erotica Can Add a Spicy Flavor to Sex

Exploring the world of erotica can be like visiting a sexy candy store of your fantasies—to savor by yourself, to share with your partner. Some people think that all sexually explicit material is pornography and that erotica and porn are cut from the same cloth. But that's not the case. What is porn and what is erotica is truly in the eye of the beholder.

The real issue at hand is for you to determine how the use of X-rated images might affect your sex life—as either a harmless pleasure or a source of resentment and disgust that could undermine your relationship. The fact is that a lot of people enjoy seeing other people having sex and enjoy getting turned on from it—usually more men than women. Still, according to researcher Ann Bridges, fully half of the women in her study said they looked at sexually explicit materials. And psychologist Meredith Chivers's study found that even though a woman may not admit or be aware of her feelings, she can be aroused by an array of explicit sexual material, including images of naked men and naked women. What makes many women object to sexually explicit materials is that they have mostly been exposed to hard-core porn. Many believe that porn is degrading to women because a porn star will do anything to please the man, and she is thrilled when he climaxes even though she doesn't have an orgasm. Not much of a thrill for most flesh-and-blood women.

Putting the merits and demerits of X-rated materials aside, most of us would agree that porn used to be, well, sleazy. But this is no longer the case. The "new school" of female-friendly erotic material is worth checking out. Erotica depicts sensual, soft-edged sexually oriented images that especially appeal to women. Most of the material— tagged as "for better couple's sex" or as a "woman's fantasy" or as "women oriented"—often shows explicit sex that is hot, but minus the hard-core edges of "old school" porn. There are endless choices about sexually explicit media. So don't be a X-rated snob.

Erotica—in any of its forms—may or may not score on your Sex-O-Meter. But if you haven't seen any, my advice is to explore it before you reject it outright. Try watching an erotic DVD /video together, one that offers the best of two worlds—what men love about sex and what women love about sex—and see what happens. What's the worst thing that can happen? You could get as sexually aroused as he gets?

After you view some of the materials, you can make an informed decision as to whether sexually explicit materials are simply one more sex toy available for you to play with or you prefer to leave it alone. In short, find your own comfort zone.

7. Sex Is Never the Same, Even with the Same Man

There are times when sex can be an intensely intimate physical and spiritual communion between you and your lover—or it can be a quick tumble in the hay or an emotional shelter in times of stress. Even a different sexual encounter with the same partner in a twenty-four-hour time period feels not like any other because of different circumstances and the nuances of intimacy. Don't be disappointed that the next time you have sex with your partner following a powerful soulful night of lovemaking it turns out to be an unemotional quickie before work.

8. Familiar Sex Is a Rewarding Classic

There is pleasure in having edgy innovative sex, and there are times when there is deep pleasure in having sex without any bells and whistles. Sex that is familiar and comforting, with him in the missionary position, both of you looking calmly into each other's eyes and telling each other that you love each other—the way you have done it too many times to count—is always like enjoying a dish of gourmet strawberry ice cream: a classic flavor that is always satisfying and tasty.

In the Meantime, If You Are Sexless in the City

You haven't met the man you passionately love until you meet him. Every woman I know wants sex to be the ultimate union of two passionate souls. In the meantime, you are facing unmet sexual desires and feeling it would be nice to have a man around once in a while. How do you deal with living in a sexual desert of involuntary celibacy with no oasis in your immediate sight?

The Date

A date isn't any one thing. It can be getting to know each other in relationship; it can be a "test" run to see if there is long term partnership potential, and it can be anything in between. For example, it can be intimate without planning a future together.

The trick to dating-with-sex and without hearing wedding bells is being realistic about not seeing you and him as a couple in your crystal ball. Most of all, don't get caught up in the wishful belief that the relationship will morph into being a passionate love given more time. Of course, because love is complex, anything is possible. Still, placing your heart and hopes on the craps table and gambling with your future may not be the best move for you.

Many women have friendly and emotionally connected dating relationships that include sex while they are looking for "the one" to come into their life. Julie, a woman in her mid-thirties, tells me she has had to make some adjustments about her expectations of dating and sex. She says, "Sometimes I get a bad case of dating fatigue, but I like sex too much to do without the option of having it in my life. Sex can sometimes be like a relief—like a good hard scratch to an itch that is driving you crazy. It can be great for reducing stress. I admit it is hard to not become disappointed when yet another date has resulted in not finding a partner. Still, I love having sex and feel more womanly when I have a sexual relationship. I think it is better to use it than lose it."

Just keep the "contract" straight, which may be an agreement to spend time together, be good friends, and have sex on occasion until such time when the relationship doesn't work for either of you anymore. If this sounds like a one-way trip to getting your hopes up and your heart broken because you know you can't handle having sex without the promise of true love coming around the corner, then don't get involved. Get back out into the dating world and find a playmate that you can passionately hold hands with as you toddle together crossing a busy street.

Hooking Up: Friends with Benefits?

You don't have any dating relationships, and you are getting restless and horny living without sex. Why not find a guy friend who is willing to be sexual partners with you? Just sex—no emotional entanglements, no dates, and no couple stuff; a friend with benefits. He's not just any guy; he's a guy you like but one you are sure you will never fall in love with (and ditto for him). You get the benefits of some nice body touching and release from sexual tension. What's the downside?

Simply, it doesn't work out for most of us. It's not the sex that makes hooking up or friends with benefits a bad bargain for many (but not all!) women—it's the nature of the deal: no emotional strings. As a gender, you are pretty much wired to desire emotional involvement with a man you have had sex with. It doesn't have to be a ring-and-a-date relationship, but it does have to have some depth of emotional attachment.

It makes more sense for a woman's soul to reserve being sexually intimate in a relationship that carries signs of mutual friendship, caring, and affection. Otherwise for most women, friends with benefits are a one-way street named *Bruised Heart*.

Speeding Down the Highway of Love

There are many different things to consider before you decide to drive off into the sunset together with a certain man. Feeling assured that you can reveal your inner vixen to him and knowing that you are cherished *and* lusted after by your partner are legitimate and healthy sides to any relationship. But one of the issues that is worth considering in your love partnership is how to handle the differences between males and females. Whether they are embedded in our DNA or are a cultural inheritance, these differences tend to dictate our lives in one way or another. Given that you want to find better ways to bond to him, in the next chapter we will tackle the challenges involved in loving and talking to a man—especially a naked man.

6

How to Talk to a Naked Man

Ever hear that men use love to get sex and women use sex to get love? Admittedly there is a grain of truth there, but mostly it's a fallacy. Women can be just as lusty as men, and men in love can be every bit as foolish, naïve, and idealistic as women. Men can get crazier about love and take more risks in the name of finding love than women. In fact, the biggest difference between men and women in dealing with passion is in their interpretation of the meaning of love within a sexual relationship. And when it comes to sex, a man can be as emotionally naked and vulnerable as he is about love, if not more so.

Here in this chapter, you'll learn about how men feel about sex, how to reach a man in ways that move you emotionally closer to him, what heats up his passionate erotic feelings for you, and what mostly turns him off.

How Men Feel About Sex

Growing up, we were taught that every man wants only one thing: to get into our pants. We learned that men lie for sex, beg for it, make fools of themselves for it. Is men's randiness a myth or a fact? Want to test the water? Just toss out a few of these kinds of questions to a mixed crowd of men and women as they are gathered together over a couple of glasses of something or other: "Are men more sexually driven than women?" "Are men always ready and willing to drop their pants any time a woman gives them the green light?" "Are men basically sex-driven creatures, which makes them putty in a woman's seductive hands?" Then stand back.

We women too often dismiss—or are unaware of—the great sexual power we wield over men. As psychologist David Buss points out, "If all women suddenly began preferring to have sex with men who walked on their hands, in a very short time half the human race would be upside down."

Sex scientists agree that while there is great variance among individual men and women, on the average men appear to think about sex and want to have sex more often than women. Men daydream more about sex and have more sexually driven images with hotter plotlines than women. Studies show that men have two and a half times the brain space devoted to sexual drive that women have. The evidence is overwhelming: men aren't from Mars; they are very sexy residents of Planet Earth.

It isn't helpful, however, to measure a man's sexual needs and emotional needs with the same yardstick you measure your needs. Kim Wallen, a behavioral scientist, thinks that we've been asking the wrong questions.

It seems we should reframe the sex drive issue by asking not about quantity and quality but specifically about how patterns of sex drives differ between men and women. Wallen argues that the primary difference between men and women is that the male sex drive is more or less continual, whereas the female sex drive is discontinuous and, in most cases, cyclical.

Still, even if you put aside the differences between our sexual desires, the fact remains that more men than women say they would rather have a quantity of sex that is available all the time, rather than high-quality sex once in a while.

Most surveys about sex find that men say they have had far more partners than women, typically two to four times as many. Either there are a bunch of phantom females out there or somebody is lying. The discrepancy may have something to do with the way men and women do the math. We tend to use different methods to calculate the number of sex partners we have had. Women tend to underestimate because they rely on a raw count, which is known to come up with less rather than more. Men use a method of rough approximation, and that is known to produce overestimation. She counts low; he counts high.

The Lesson of the Porcupine

Despite the fact that sex is a major part of a man's life, sex therapist Ian Kerner says, "Most guys know more about what is under the hood of the car than under the hood of a clitoris." True enough. Many men could benefit from some basic lessons about male and female anatomy, especially how women respond sexually and what makes sex more pleasurable for us. However, be warned: teaching Sex Ed. 101 to your lover is easier said than done.

If you want to have more passionate—more physical and more emotionally connected—sex with your partner, you'll need to tiptoe lightly into that territory, because you are in danger of walking on very thin ice.

Sex is a man's primary proving ground—the arena where he evaluates himself as a man. Talking with a man about his and your sex life—unless it is to gush over how much you love having sex with him—requires great tact. Avoid the temptation to put your dissatisfaction on the table—even if you are being nonjudgmental about whose "fault it is." I'm cool to the advice from experts encouraging women to straightforwardly "communicate with their partner" about their unfulfilled sexual hopes and dreams.

Count to a hundred at least five times before you say anything out loud to your partner about not being sexually satisfied. And start counting again. Think about it: what makes you think that a sexual powwow can solve the problems appearing nightly in your bed? In fact, I advise you not to flat out bring up the dynamics of your sex life for a "talk," especially in the bed. Even if you are on your very best sweetie-pie behavior, talking about the downside of your sex life is not an aphrodisiac.

It's not that your desires and expectations for passionately emotional and physically passionate connections aren't legitimate; they are. Of course you can, and should, discuss your concerns about your sex life with the man in your sex life. No need to pretend that all is well when it isn't. Silence doesn't solve anything; in fact it is likely to make the dissatisfaction you feel fester and eventually lead to resentment and more dissatisfaction. But there is a way to bring up your desire for an improved sex life illustrated by a very old joke:

"How do two porcupines make love?"

Answer: "Very carefully."

No matter how gently you deliver the message about your desire to increase the heat or deepen the intimate connection when you have sex, he is likely to feel that you are hitting him below the belt, unfairly and literally. You are directing attention to one of his most vulnerable spots—his sexual prowess.

For a woman to really comprehend what makes a man tick sexually, she has, to be blunt, to come to grips with the relationship of a man to his penis. It is a relationship like no other, one that gives a man great pleasure, one that is a source of pride—it is the very core of his manliness. Yet, at the same time, it is a relationship of insecurity about measuring up to other men and to your expectations and one that creates, at a deep level, worries about his ability to perform. Thus, never speak ill of the penis.

It is understandable that if things in the bedroom hit an awkward moment that has to do with his erection, or lack thereof, you might be tempted to tell a joke or try to say something "funny" to make light of the situation. Don't do it. He will fail to appreciate your attempts to put a humorous twist on what is usually humiliating to him.

Bill, a guy attending a workshop in Phoenix, offered this advice: "When he is having trouble, don't try to get all cute with the baby talk or do what my ex-girlfriend did to me— she gave my penis a pet name. Not funny. I did say 'ex'-girlfriend, right? Just get busy with more foreplay, and with some luck his penis may wake up and come to the party."

Returning to the porcupines, you'll find that when porcupines feel threatened their quills pump up in preparation for going on the attack or to defend themselves. Men are like that (I know you can say the same about many women, but we are talking specifically about men's defensive mechanisms here). If he feels that you are being critical of him as a lover, a man can put up a defensive shield as effective as the porcupine's pointed quills are at keeping the enemy at bay. When faced with hearing words uttered from the lips of the man you love, expressing his disappointment in your love-making skills, you would feel defensive and maybe puff out a few quills too, wouldn't you?

What Turns Men On?

What many women fail to understand about male sexuality is this: men are a lot more sexually complicated than they are usually portrayed. Their sexual desires and sexual prowess are influenced by any number of factors just as women's sexual libido is sensitive to many different factors. There are different opinions about what makes a man's sexual energy kick in, but there is agreement that a man's sexual libido is closely tied to his levels of testosterone, his sense of sexual confidence, and the opportunity to have sex with a woman he finds sexually enticing. Adding to that mix are other less recognized but powerful influences.

Adrenaline Fuels a Man's Sex Drive

Feeling anxiety about being in a dicey situation or feeling a sense of danger can pump up our adrenaline, resulting in a higher pulse rate, harder breathing, and sweating palms—the same signs of sexual arousal. And men, more than women, are affected by those jolts of adrenaline. It seems that for him, being in a fear/anxiety adrenaline-producing situation sets off a sexually charged chain reaction and heightens his sexual attraction to a specific woman.

For evidence, we travel to a famous experiment called the "Shaky Bridge," which involved setting up men to walk across two different bridges. One bridge was a suspension bridge made of wooden slats and suspended by a wire, hanging hundreds of feet over a deep river gorge. It swayed back and forth when a person walked on the bridge, making for some queasy moments crossing it. The other bridge was solid and stable and elevated only about ten feet above ground. As the subjects (single men between the ages of nineteen and twenty-five) walked across each bridge (on different days), they were met by an attractive woman research assistant. She asked each man to fill out a short questionnaire and write a short essay in response to a picture he was shown (the picture was from the Thematic Apperception Test, which relates to sexual imagery). After he finished the task, each man was thanked and invited to give the assistant a call at home if he wanted more information about the study.

The men who walked across the wobbly bridge used more sexual imagery than did the men from the solid bridge and were more likely to call the assistant later at her home to ask her out. Which means? According to this research (and other studies that followed), there are links between the rush of adrenaline—whether it comes from a great run around the track or from being in a scary situation—and getting sexually turned on. Most important, it helps explain why men love to have spontaneous sex, especially in offbeat places or where discovery is a possibility.

Variety for a Man Is the Spice of Sex

Having sex with a variety of women, or with more than one woman at the same time, is the stuff of many men's sexual fantasies. Given that you might not be up for inviting a harem over for a tryst, what's a girl to do? Take heart. There are many ways to keep your sex life from feeling like a version of *Groundhog Day*. To help light a fire under your imagination and his, check out some of the many really good books and media on the specifics of how to stimulate a man's mind and body and heat up both your libido and his (see my recommendations in the back of the book). Keep in mind that whatever brings out your inner vixen is what turns him on the most. And there is a bonus here: when he gets passionately aroused, you are the beneficiary. It is a win-win situation.

When His Libido Is Downshifted

Women are generally cast as the gender with low libido, and men are generally cast as the sexually rejected and frustrated counterpart. So it is baffling to a woman when the man in her life who has always been sexually responsive becomes suddenly disinterested in sex. When, more than a few times, he rolls over and turns out the light despite your overtures about wanting sex, such as showing off your hot new teddy, you are likely to see his lack of passion as your personal failure. As a woman, you point the finger of blame at yourself: "He must be having an affair." "I knew it; I'm too fat." "He doesn't love me anymore." None of this self-doubt will get you anywhere. There is no point in playing the blame game. For starters, he isn't all that unusual. There are more than a few good men out there in Lust Land with low levels of sexual desire. Ian Kerner, the sex therapist mentioned a little earlier and author of *He Comes Next: The Thinking Woman's Guide to Pleasuring a Man*, says that in his practice he sees a growing number of men who have lower sex drives than their female partners. Kerner explains: "There are no firm statistics on this, but many therapists will tell you that low male desire is a silent epidemic." No wonder low desire in men is America's best-kept secret. Too many men are reluctant to reach out for help because not being sexually "ready" is a mark against their mythical manhood.

Before your sex-iffy relationship slides into a sex-starved one, you need to become aware of what could be negatively affecting his lust for sex—from stress at work to worry about aging parents, money problems, a change in his hormones, (this may sting) boredom with your sex life together, or a reaction to your crabby attitude toward him. Let's peel that onion by taking a closer look at the usual suspects behind a man's flagging desire to have sex.

Testosterone, Testosterone, Testosterone

We know about the influence of women's Byzantine hormones on our sex lives, including the dreaded PMS, the frantic surges from the onset of menopause to the end of menopause, and the teeter-totter of hormones during pregnancy and after childbirth. But "andropause," the gradual series of hormonal changes due to aging that men experience starting in their twenties and thirties, shows up on fewer radar screens.

These changing levels of testosterone affect almost all men by creating a downward shift in sexual libido and in the ability to have sex the way men are used to having sex. It will probably take longer for them to achieve an erection and an intermission for them to get another one to partake in Act Two. As midlife progresses, almost all men have some difficulty getting and sustaining an erection, known as *ED* (*erectile dysfunction*) each time they have sex. In addition to the waning of testosterone, smoking or the use of antidepressants (especially selective serotonin reuptake inhibitors) may lower a man's sex drive because some medications can dampen libido and the capacity to partake in sex from start to finish.

Before you consider stampeding out the door to his doctor's office to get a supply of testosterone, be aware of some caveats. First, once average levels of testosterone are reached, there is not much that can be gained by increasing levels further. Second, there is a "chicken and egg" thing here: testosterone increases sex drive and sexual activity, which in turn increases the levels of testosterone. More or less, it's "use it or lose it."

Fear of Failure

Worrying about a recent less-than-stellar sexual performance contributes mightily to a man's lack of enthusiasm for having sex. We are all aware that a woman can fake her sexual responses, especially orgasms (a tip of the hat to Meg Ryan). Conversely, it is virtually impossible for a man to fake "coming." Some men report having a climax (ejaculating) but not experiencing the release and euphoria of an orgasm. There is a fine point between "coming" and "orgasm," one not readily apparent. If you see or feel semen, you might assume he has had an orgasm. But that might not be the case. Men rarely confide in women the fact that they weren't completely sexually satisfied.

If a woman has a less-than-thrilling sexual experience, she usually doesn't internalize it or see it as a sign that her sexual life is diminished. We rarely are embarrassed about it or even dwell on it. We may be disappointed, even frustrated, but we tend to move on and look ahead to the next time, when it will be better. Not so with most men.

Each time he is unable to achieve an erection, each time his partner doesn't come, each time sex is more blah than exciting becomes etched into his memory log. Those negative experiences can inhibit his desire to have sex, at least for a while. Psychologist Regan Gurung says, "When a man is feeling insecure about his sexual performance, he'll come up with as many excuses as he can not to have sex. He might suddenly start spending more time surfing the Internet. He might stay at work late more often, or he might watch TV while telling his wife, 'You go on to bed.' "

The Scales of Desire

As I said before, men are visual creatures. They become sexually aroused by what they see, especially a woman's body (just check out men's magazines). A woman doesn't have to be thin to be a sex goddess to most men, but she needs not to have too much meat on those bones. Although some men love big women, most men are not attracted to a woman who is carrying considerable body fat. I know, we hate hearing that. You could feel offended and, frankly, get a bit uppity, about the audacity of men to judge the sexual desirability of a woman based on her weight. I grant you that it feels morally indefensible, but it is a fact of life. (I think women feel the same about the sexual attractiveness of overweight men, but we tend to be less judgmental and less up-front about it). Sara, a woman I met at my seminar in San Francisco, stayed behind to share with me her "fat" story: "A few years ago I was with the man in my life at an airport in anticipation of a wonderful romantic getaway week together. I hadn't seen him in nine weeks, and I was antsy with the desire to be with him. After we found seats in the waiting area, I went off to take a bathroom break. As I walked back to where he was sitting, I became aware that he was looking at me in a 'pained' way. I sat down, and he took my hands in his and said very sweetly, 'I'll support you in every single way it takes to help you lose weight. I know it is difficult to lose weight, but I'm here for you. It would mean a lot to me if we could work together to help you lose this extra weight you've put on.' And he very sincerely added, 'I know you would feel better about yourself,' and gave me a reassuring hug. I was speechless, mortified. I admit I had put on some pounds. I wasn't happy about it, hated looking in a mirror, and was feeling self-conscious. But did he have take on the role of the fat police and bring it up before we even checked into our hotel? To say his 'I'm here for you, Chunko Lady' session put a cold wet blanket on any hot vacation sex is an understatement. I know he didn't mean to hurt me, but I couldn't wait for the week to end. In my mind I kept replaying a mental video of him appraising my expanded tush as I walked away from him. That was the end of that relationship, but I still think about him and feel the hurt from his comments about my weight. I've taken a lot of the weight off and sometimes think about sending him my now-sorta-slender-self picture with a note. But it isn't worth it. My weight would be a wedge issue." Was Sara unfair to him? Probably. Actually, yes.

Be assured that a man may not fall out of love with a woman who has gained considerable weight (above and beyond pregnancy or a medical condition), but he may be less sexually attracted to her. On the other hand, a man's weight, especially a weight gain that has produced the "beer gut," may play a role in his lack of libido. If he feels out of shape, he is likely to lack the confidence to take the sexual initiative. When you take inventory of what is causing a man's diminished sexual drive, you need to assess whether weight (yours and/or his) has become a silent coconspirator.

The Bitch Factor

A woman's critical, unappreciative attitude toward a man outside of the bedroom shuts down his sexual desire for her in the bedroom. Secretly or overtly, many women regard their partners as fixer-upper projects, rather like run-down property that shows some promise but needs a lot of work. The dark side of this picky and slightly superior attitude of hers toward him is that he ends up feeling unloved or disrespected for who he is. If you run roughshod over his need to be appreciated, he may not say much, but the damage done to your passionately sensual relationship with him will speak volumes.

Igniting the Fires Within

If sex seems to have fallen into the same-old, same-old and is losing its fiery glow, or if his—or your—sexual desires seem to have shifted into low gear, don't wait around for your fairy godmother to appear with magic erotic dust to reenergize them. On a playful seduction level, here are a few of the many ways you can stir those embers and spice up what happens in your bedroom besides sleeping.

Rattle His Sexual Cage

From time to time, men need to get all shook up about sex. So surprise him with sensually edgy seduction scenarios. For example, consider your bedroom a stage. Get his attention (turn off all of his remote and hand-held electronic devices), play some sexy music, and put on a private show with you playing the lead role of an erotic adults-only dancer (minus those weird platform shoes). Basically, slowly undress with an attitude. Start by stripping off the outer layer, say, those gray sweats, to the next layer of racy or lacy lingerie, to something that just barely covers nipples and your mons veneris. Begging him to take it off—take it all off of you—is an irresistible invitation. If you would feel ridiculous grinding out a striptease, do something else. Anything you are comfortable doing—anything that works to lift your sex life out of the doldrums. You don't have to be a dominatrix in leather thigh-highs cracking a whip or have the body of a swimsuit-model-of-the-month to get his sexual motor revved up; just be focused on giving and receiving sexual pleasure. What turns him on the most is you being turned on, and what turns you on the most is having him turned on to you. It is a win-win situation.

Pass the Popcorn

As I have mentioned before, being the visual beings they are, most men love pornography. The problem is, as we also discussed before, many women don't. The solution isn't to censor him but to expand your erotic education. Don't be put off if he gets his sex "on" button pushed by watching the films—accept that he's feeling sexy and wants to have sex with you; that's a good thing.

Now, I'm talking about porno/erotica as an occasional way to keep your sex life interesting, not as the only way he can get aroused. That's a different issue, one that calls for a therapist. (Check out my referrals in the back of the book.) If you really can't get into using commercial porno/erotica media as sex toys, maybe the two of you can star in your own sexy video for your private viewing pleasure. But that's a big step and one that requires trust and your being the keeper of the tape.

Don't Talk—Do

Remember hearing "Actions speak louder than words"? When it comes to men and sex, that advice is golden. Men respond to show and touch, not talk. Take away any pressure on him to "talk" about sex by sharing passionate, intimate sex with him in a nonverbal way. Let your fingers do the walking—reach out and touch him. Men love to be touched. They crave hugs, especially body hugs. For many men (and many women), sex by itself is how they communicate feeling intimately connected. Plus it's good to know that oxytocin, the bonding hormone, is released in the brain after a twenty-second hug from a partner—and triggers the brain's trust center. Not only a bonus for him but one for you as well.

Try a Little Tenderness

How hard is that? You love the guy, right? Men, to a much greater degree than women, thrive on being appreciated. A man blossoms—as a plant does when watered—when you let him know that you love him for being the sexy kind of guy he is. Folk wisdom says, "You catch more flies with honey than vinegar."

In other words, people will be drawn to you if you talk sweetly to them and fly away if you speak to them with sour words. It certainly is true about men: they need a lot of honey. I'm not talking about giving a man cheesy compliments as a form of manipulation. The "honey" must be heartfelt and sincere. My point is that what happens outside of the bedroom has a great effect on what happens inside the bedroom. It is hard to shift gears from being upset or angry to being loving and intimate.

Hit the Pause Button

If, after a few months, your seduction and sexy moves haven't boosted the passionate energy between you, now the silence can be broken. It is time to have a gentle conversation about what is happening and mostly not happening. If this downshift in his libido or yours is happening for reasons that you can't identify, the next step is for each of you to visit a health practitioner for a physical checkup and then, for both of you as a couple, to see a certified sex therapist. Think of taking action to improve your sex life as opening the door to cultivating a deeper understanding of your sexual desires—his and yours—and to learn new ways of expressing your sensual, passionate feelings for each other.

Running with Pharmaceutically Enhanced Wolves

If he is having problems with having the kind of sex he wants to have, and a physical exam says all is well, it wouldn't be unusual for his clinician to discuss a prescription of Viagra, those "little blue pills"—or newer drugs such as Levitra and Cialis—the kinds of sexual enhancement "Magic Pills" that are advertised constantly. Originally, the ads targeted men over age fifty, offering them (and their partners) a pharmaceutical way to overcome ED. So I was taken aback when on the TV show "Rescue Me," Sheila asked Tommy (a guy who appears to be in his thirties), "Are you taking one of those cock pills? I've never seen you like this! We've been doing this for hours!" Tommy responds (hurt look on face), "No, babe, this is au naturel for you. All for you." Denial aside, Sheila's suspicions were later confirmed; and this is not an isolated incidence.

Apparently, pharmaceutical enhancements to increase a man's sexual capacity are being used by younger men who aren't actually experiencing ED but who use the enhancements for an "extra" boost. And for older men, drugs like Viagra, Cialis, and Levitra are now the mass panacea for a flagging sex drive or to light up sexual fireworks. Ready or not, this tidal wave of sexual aids is affecting men's and women's relationships, inside and outside of the bedroom.

For some women, the idea of having sex with a man who is using some kind of pharmaceutical aid to have an erection, or to have a stronger erection, or to be interested in having sex at all, is a major turn-off. They believe they should be enough of an aphrodisiac. For other women, the aids are a gift from the gods. No matter how you feel about them, pharmaceutical sex aids for men are now a fact of life for him and therefore for you.

Sex, Actually

The most important thing to know about sex is that it is an essential part of a loving passionate relationship. We get pleasure from many different things—art, music, dancing, sunsets, sunrises—but sex is a unique and compelling pleasure. It is how you connect to him and how he connects to you, physically and emotionally. Sex is the touchstone between you and the man you love, and it is different each time you have sex. You are never the exact same person each time you have sex. He is never the exact same person with you each time you have sex with him. Sex is about two different people coming together at the intersection between love and intimacy. And, for a man, sex is ultimate intimacy.

The Dark Side
of Passion

7

Alone Together

Breathing Spaces and Setting Love's Boundaries

Sharing a bed with the man you love passionately is great. Sharing the rest of the home and everything else called life—sometimes not so much. There are lovers who build a love nest and place it on the highest hill like a medieval castle and enjoy the coziness or the isolation of being together. For others, being joined at the hip is just too confining. If either you or he feels on the edge of being suffocated by too much togetherness or kept out in the cold, sexual passion becomes vulnerable and often impossible.

Boundary issues are not only the pebble in the shoe of committed relationships; they can be the cause of problems that end a promising relationship. The differences in each person's need for "togetherness" emerge as a relationship becomes serious, but too often these issues are brushed aside in the glow of being in love and thus aren't dealt with in an up-front and honest way.

In this chapter we focus on ways to set boundaries— whether you are on your way to a passionate love or are already there—that deepen your passionate partnership without poking a hole in anyone's love balloon. You'll learn how to come to agreements and honor each other's needs for breathing space to be alone as individuals and yet together as a couple.

Stand Back from the Rope

Although we cling to the notion that two people in love somehow become "one," that idea is a myth. In all passionate relationships, over time and to varying degrees, you can count on a boundary issue's emerging. The following are comments from women who say that while they are passionately in love, there are times when they feel smothered in their relationship.

- "I love him, but at times I just wish I could be alone for a while. Not only physically but to have more 'mental space.' "
- "There are times I fantasize about checking into a hotel so I can have a king-size bed all to myself and not have to see all of his stuff around."
- "I like to have privacy in the bathroom—he says I'm too uptight—but I just think there are some things that are off-limits."
- "I hate having to ask him what he is thinking all the time, but he doesn't offer much. He says he doesn't have any secrets, but I wonder what's going on in there."

Anything sound familiar? Dealing with differences between you and your partner as to what is reasonable and "normal" about sharing and about drawing boundaries around privacy and property can be a major bump in the road. Sharing bed and board and a deep emotional connection means you can't hide much from each other. And because of this close proximity, you shouldn't be surprised if what was his charming little beauty mark now takes on the appearance of a giant unsightly mole. If you don't face up to the reality that you two differ on the issue of privacy, you'll trudge along OK for a while, but eventually one of you, or both of you, will feel invaded or catch a cold from the arctic air of rejection. One thing you can count on, no matter which side of the property line you're speaking from, is that you'll both feel misunderstood or angry and frustrated.

Defining the "We" in "You and Me"

Let's define what "boundaries" are. Rochelle, a counselor attending one of my workshops, gives us a definition: "A healthy, well-established boundary is an internalized line (physical, emotional, intellectual) that enhances your sense of identity by implanting more deeply the precious knowledge that you are a separate human being." For some people, boundaries are defined as "breathing space"—a sense of being in one's own solitary emotional turf; for others it is "living space"—their property and how the household is managed. It's not unusual for one partner to believe that being a couple comes with a "right to know" clause attached, meaning the right to know everything about each other—hopes for your future, secrets about the past, and the good, the bad, and the ugly things that occur in thought and in action every day. If both of you are on the same mental wavelength about what boundaries are and are not, then you have no problem. To use a business metaphor, if, however, one of you is merger-hungry and the other is merger-wary, you should be prepared for a crash in the market.

Defining what is "us" and what is "I" and what is "you" is at the core of the issue. The boundaries per se aren't really the problem. It is how you and your partner deal with them. This much is for sure: agreeing to boundaries that make each person feel like a cherished and equal partner goes a long way in dealing with a passionate partnership's tribulations large and small.

Avoid Drawing the Line in the Sand

It is possible to have the right impulse about protecting your privacy and at the same time take the wrong action to solve the problem. Straightforwardly communicating to your partner that you are feeling cramped and saying it in a way that is free from being irate isn't easy. Too often we lash out at him, finding flaws in his privacy issues, rather than seeing the privacy issue as our own. Putting up a barrier—one that is a mental model of the Great Wall of China—can cut us off from the people we care about. All you may need is to draw a loving line in the sand. Cynthia, a UNESCO worker, tells me she found herself doing just that—building walls when all it took was some simple understanding. "Max, my husband of one whole year, is a cuddly kind of man. I like that about him, but I felt overwhelmed by his need to hug me a couple times a day, especially when I was busy doing something. Usually I would snap at him to leave me alone. Other times I'd get really peeved at him because I felt he wasn't hearing me say that I would prefer not to be hugged at that moment. Finally we got into a few of those accusatory 'You are too cold'–'You are too needy' arguments. He would get a hurt puppy look on his face, and I would feel guilty, which made me even more upset. The weekends became especially uneasy. Finally, over a tense Sunday breakfast, we finally were able to talk about what was making us unhappy. He said he felt deserted because when I was home I was preoccupied with work. I travel a lot, and it was true that when I was home I had my face buried in the computer for hours. All he wanted, he said, was to feel connected beyond the times we had sex. I told him I did enjoy his affectionate persona but there were times when I felt he was being overbearing and not respecting my feelings. He came up with a solution to what he called the 'not so much hugging' issue. He said, 'OK, I won't hug you unless I'm invited to, but you can hug me anytime you feel like it!' After a day of him backing off, I found I missed those spontaneous hugs. I finally got it. He felt insecure about us. So I made a big deal of hugging him and telling him I loved him. We had some good laughs over who was hugging whom more. The tension melted away. I know he understands now that although I love him, I need to have more elbow room. And I have come to be more understanding that he needs me to show him more affection and attention."

Cynthia's experience illustrates how boundary mismatches can be resolved. It helps to wait for the right time to talk about what is happening between you and to address one thing at a time. Essentially, you can avoid conflict by learning how to balance each other's needs for separateness and closeness and honing your skills in the art of negotiation and compromise.

Setting Boundaries

You and Your Comfort Zone

Begin with tuning in to your own comfort zone, a place where you are who you are in terms of how much "space"— i.e., autonomy—you need or don't need. If you aren't sure of how you define "space," how can he possibly be expected to respond to what you need? For instance, do you mean an hour by yourself after you get home after work? Do you mean hands off of your computer and CDs? Or do you mean you want to watch—all by yourself—the movies you love and he doesn't? Or do you mean you want to tell him "Don't even go there about my sister"? Think through what your boundary issues are before you put them out on the table. You don't have to be able to articulate the fine points of your expectations as if you were drawing up a contract. It does help, though, to have a good general idea of what bugs you in terms of togetherness and what doesn't and then to be able to define what you need. Consider this: asking for what you want increases your chances of getting it!

Wear Your Party Manners

Be open and agreeable about carving out ways to love and honor each other's desires to be individuals within the coziness of being together. This means laying out rules for discussing the parameters around sharing home and hearth (and everything else). And this means fighting fair: no digs, no blowing up, no changing the subject, no bringing up things that you know are his soft spots (his mother, his job, his team's having lost the office softball game). Never underestimate the power of simply being nice, kind, and considerate. John Gottman, a psychology professor at the University of Washington, and his colleagues discovered that relationships hang on the number of kind and unkind interactions; when the ratio falls below five to one, expect to hear the sounds of a siren warning that a breakup is approaching.

Address Needs Rather than "Rights"

Both of you should have an equal opportunity to be who you are. Make it clear that your desire to set boundaries is a deeply felt need, not a whim. Don't get emotional; be matter-of-fact. Don't let boundary discussions turn into a tumultuous tug-of-war over who has the greater boundary issues and therefore the greater needs. The approach that works best is to lay out what you need, let your partner talk about what he needs, and then discuss to find a solution that works for both of you. In short, put the focus on "why" you feel the way you do and not on demanding your inalienable rights. For example, simply stating, "I need to be alone to sort out my thoughts or I get lost in an emotional maze" is a nicer way to put it than "I need you to go away and not bother me so I can have time by myself." Coming to a mutual agreement before the well of good feelings between you becomes poisoned is obviously important. For one thing, it frees up your creative energy and opens the door to experiencing greater intimacy and passion as lovers who appreciate each other as unique individuals.

Be a Bit Mysterious

Setting boundaries around sharing inner thoughts is just as important to some people as setting physical boundaries around their "stuff." If that's you, don't berate yourself for not being comfortable with a "letting it all hang out" style of sharing. In fact, being a bit mysterious has its advantages. Richard, a landscape designer in Taos, New Mexico, says that nothing is sexier than a woman who has a sense of reserve about her. "A woman who carries an aura of mystery about her is very intriguing—it draws me to her and makes me want to know more about her. I like slowly putting together the puzzle of who she is, one piece at a time."

You can be emotionally intimate and share confidential thoughts with the man you love, and at the same time you can have a separate emotional life, one that is not fused into him. Think about it—you do it all the time with your girlfriends and close family members. You share your thoughts and dreams and keep the window open into your inner vulnerable self. Yet you don't share every single thought—you keep some things to yourself. The idea is to be open and connected to others, while minding the private garden of your mind.

When He Wants More Space

If your partner tells you that he needs more space—even if he says it nicely—hearing "Back off!" in any form is never music to our ears. It feels like a betrayal of the intimacy that we thought we shared. Joyce, an architect in Charleston, tells me that she has a vivid memory of being in love but kept at arm's length. "I was head over heels in love with a wonderful man. Unfortunately, he lived in Seattle, three time zones away from Charleston, but we went back and forth a lot. We were celebrating the 'one year ago we met' day over a long weekend and took a walk along the Ashley River. We stopped to sit in the sun and enjoy the glorious fall weather. Out of the blue, he told me that he was feeling totally smothered—'hammered'—by my expectations for our relationship. He assured me that he loved me. But he felt I was pushing way too much togetherness stuff on him. It was a bitter blow. He capped it off by telling me that our visits were too close together for him; he couldn't take that much time off from work anymore. He was adamant that he didn't want the relationship to end, but he needed to have more time to himself. I assured him that I understood, which I didn't. I was actually dumbfounded. I thought he loved the 'love stuff'—the 'Love ya' morning e-mails, the evening 'How was your day?' phone calls, and the sexy and sweet cards we sent each other—as much as I did. I told him I would respect his wishes. And I tried. Over the next three years, I thought twice before I picked up the phone to call him. We still spoke a couple of times a week, but I missed the joy of being in touch daily. We had been seeing each other about every six weeks, now it was stretching to three, even four months. He was as passionate as ever when we were together. But I was under a lot of strain trying to pretend I was just fine with our agreement. I began tiptoeing around him when we were together—and felt relieved when the visit ended. Looking back, I now know I felt abandoned. I wanted to be a much-attached couple, a couple who shared an easiness about being loving and close. Mostly I harbored the distressing feeling, even though he never said so, that he thought I was flawed, overly needy. Eventually, with a wounded heart, I ended it."

Joyce went on to say, "The strangest thing was how surprised he was when I did end it. He told me he thought I was fine with everything. By then it was too late for me to put any energy into mending the relationship. I should have been more up-front about hating being so unattached and distant, because I was putting a lid on my true nature. Instead I made the mistake of believing it had to be 'his way or the highway.' It turned out that it probably wasn't all that nonnegotiable."

Joyce's story rings sadly familiar for many of us because it illustrates a universal truth. Some of us have a hunger for closeness, and others prefer to keep a bit of a distance, to have a dollop of autonomy. You can cross your fingers and hope that the man you love, your soul mate, shares your beliefs about being emotionally and physically close. Maybe he does. And maybe he doesn't. In either case, no one is inherently right or wrong. The best thing you can do is to positively deal with the issue.

Dealing with Wide-Open Spaces

What can you do when the man in your life says he needs "space"? Put your energy into creating innovative ways to arrive at mutually agreed-on decisions about what will work for you and what will work for him. As Don Miguel Ruiz, in his elegant book *The Four Agreements*, wisely advises: "Find the courage to ask questions and to express what you really want. Communicate with others as clearly as you can to avoid misunderstandings, darkness, and drama. With just this one agreement, you can completely transform your life."

Don't Fence Him In

That rickety construct that is the male self-image doesn't want to think of himself as a prisoner of love but rather as a free agent. If he has set firm boundaries around how much intimacy he can tolerate 24/7, don't expect him to change. A man puts up his protective shield when a woman takes on the persona of a mind detective—probing him to respond to a battery of questions on the order of "What are you thinking?" Part of the problem is that women, more often than men, tend to confuse the desire for intimacy and being close with their partner with the need to put into words their every thought and their every emotion and then expect an equally intimate sharing from their partner. It is a setup for frustration and ultimately failure. You have to meet him where he is. Instead of bugging him to let you jump over his emotional fence, relax. You may be surprised that once you stop pushing for more intimacy he stops pushing back.

Give the Guy a Moment

If you are the one with more of an urge to merge, you won't get more closeness by insisting on it, demanding it, or whining about the lack of it. It is a mistake to use your feminine ploys to make him feel guilty about wanting to be alone (either mentally or physically) for a while. Forget about trying to worm out of him just what "a while" means. Don't roll over to old fears that when a man says "I need space" it is actually is a typical commitment phobia maneuver. Most likely the guy just needs a moment. He may be in a foul mood, one that has nothing to do with you. Don't take it personally. This much I can tell you: every man I've met through my seminars talks about how much he appreciates it when his partner doesn't "freak out" when he wants to have some time to himself. Because he expresses the need for more space doesn't mean he no longer loves you. In short, don't overreact to his need to have some privacy. As my mother used to tell me, "Don't throw the baby out with the bathwater." Consider that just as you are entitled to defining "my space," your partner has the inalienable right to his own private thoughts, how he spends his time, his choice in friends, and his taste in clothes. Get my drift?

Freeze-Frame and Breathe

Let's say you aren't certain whether his boundary needs are just that or a signal that he is on his way out the door. The grating truth may be, as the bestselling book astutely put it, "He's just not that into you."

In addition to paying close attention to his actual behavior, consider evaluating the situation by doing something that pulls you out of the spinning spirals of confusing emotions. Try this: practice Freeze-Frame, a stress prevention technique designed by the Institute of HeartMath. The technique is based on the Zen-sounding concept of "Be still to know." You simply allow yourself to become very still inside and mentally frame the issue. To make the Freeze-Frame approach even more effective, combine it with BREATHE, a decision-making model used by the Pecos River Learning Center outside of Santa Fe: (1) Stop. Take time out. Separate yourself from your surroundings and breathe in deeply, hold, and slowly exhale. Repeat until calm and focused. (2) Gently challenge your assumptions. Ask yourself, "What's real?" "What seems false?" Envision the situation from all angles. Can you form images of what might be the worst outcome? The best? (3) Then concentrate on the area around your heart, generating a positive feeling. Using your intuition, ask your heart for an answer to this perplexing situation. Stay focused and listen to what your heart says. Put both your observations about how he acts and what your heart tells you into the same decision-making pot and go from there.

Summing Up: We Are Always Alone Together

Struggling to cultivate your passionate intradependence and still find the *me* in the *we* may feel like a twenty-first century dilemma, but it isn't. It's been going on for a long, long time. We can all take heart, and take home some good advice, from Kahlil Gibran's *The Prophet*. I grant you it is in danger of being written off as a cliché because it suffers from too many saccharine recitations at far too many tearfully sentimental weddings. Putting all that aside, Gibran's words still elegantly point us in the right direction:

But let there be spaces in your togetherness,
And let the winds of the heavens dance between you.
Sing and dance together and be joyous, but let
each one of you be alone. . . .

The potent message here is this: no matter how deep the passionate intensity between you and your lover, or how much you finish each other's sentences and anticipate each other's needs, *you are alone as you are together.* Two people can never merge into one emotional being. Enjoy the tempo and flow and ebb of being together and being alone. Just like Ginger and Fred, you'll find that some of the fun of being a couple is dancing to the rhythm of merging and then lightly stepping apart. Sway to the sound of the drums or shake your bootie—whatever expresses the beat of your heart.

8

Jealousy

The Green-Eyed Monster
and You

Imagine you are at a party. Across the room, your partner is talking intently with an attractive woman. She occasionally leans toward him, smiles, and touches his arm, and they have a good laugh. He leans toward her and whispers something in her ear. They walk out to the dance floor, where they obviously enjoying dancing with each other.

What would you be feeling? Happy to see him having a good time? Perhaps a tad jealous? Perhaps more than a tad? Here's some more information. That woman is a famous artist and is devilishly pretty. Still happy to see him enjoying himself? Now, one more detail: the woman is your partner's older sister. Does that change everything? It did for almost every woman that has ever attended my seminars.

Be honest. Did your antenna go up at the thought of your partner showing interest in another woman? Or are you not able to imagine a situation where you would feel jealous?

How would you feel if your partner never showed the slightest twinge of jealousy over you? Disappointed? Glad? Not an issue?

This may surprise you, but jealousy isn't "one" emotion—it is a cluster of confusing and often conflicting emotions, and not a one is about being passionately in love. In this chapter, we'll uncover the many faces of jealousy and what triggers those emotions. You'll learn how to cope constructively if that green-eyed monster should raise its ugly head. And it might, because as much as you and your partner passionately love each other, you can't build a barbed-wire fence around your relationship to keep out unwanted intruders (say, a flirty co-worker in the office) or unpleasant surprises (the ex who moved back into town).

What Is That Green-Eyed Monster Doing in Your Passionate Psyche?

Jealousy and envy are often spoken about in the same breath as if they're interchangeable emotions. They aren't. They are very different emotions with different MOs. Envy is longing for another's personality or physical looks, talents, wealth or other earthly goods, or status in life. In contrast, jealousy is always about sex—actually, a sexual triangle—a real or imagined threat to your intimate relationship posed by a rival who is trying to lure your lover away in the dark of night. Or at the office party. We envy someone when we wish we had what they have. We become jealous when we fear someone wants what we have: our man.

What adds to the confusion about how jealousy plays out in a relationship is our changing cultural ideas about it. Back in the 1950s through the 1960s, jealousy was considered a normal way to prove one's love. In the 1970s and 1980s, jealousy was frowned on as an unhealthy state of insecurity and a show of a lack of trust in your partner. One of the earmarks of the so-called Hippie Movement was the emphasis on not "owning anyone," thus eliminating the need for jealousy. This was, of course, to put it mildly, not particularly successful. Now fast-forward to the twenty-first century. Jealousy, when acknowledged at all, is greeted with ambivalence. On one hand it is considered a personality flaw (paranoia mostly), and on the other the outcome of unbridled passion. Putting pop culture aside, what do we know about jealousy except that it is commonly and universally referred to as "the green-eyed monster"? There are psychologists who say that jealousy is a cover for feelings such as inadequacy, insecurity, and a fear of abandonment. Masquerading as passion, jealousy is a form of control, they claim, a way to keep one's partner hostage. Other scientists insist that jealousy is a "natural" emotional response to being in a passionate relationship because it is the living legacy of long-running genetic conflicts about love and sex between men and women. Jealous thoughts and feelings arise from negative and confused states of hurt, anger, and fear. Despite those differences of opinion, there is one thing we all agree on: even in its least destructive mode, jealousy fuels the fires of upheaval and distrust between you and the man you love. And if you let it, even a dab of jealousy can turn into a full-blown bout of suspicion and distrust, which, in turn, is guaranteed to squeeze the joy out of your passionate feelings for each other.

What Triggers the Green-Eyed Monster Within You?

What, if anything, would make you become possessed by the green-eyed monster? Consider this: jealousy depends on three things. One, your perception that your relationship is threatened by a rival who possesses traits you admire but think you lack. Two, the amount of trust you have in your partner's disinterest in being lured away. Three, your confidence in yourself as a woman worthy of being passionately loved and cherished. In the end, jealousy is fed by a shaky sense of self-confidence and a worry that you don't have many options out there on the "mate market." What can help calm the jealous soul is to face up to what is making you feel so rotten, so unglued. Psychologist Harriet Lerner offers this advice: "When we can't fully face our anxiety and clarify its sources, we tend to act it out instead. . . . We owe it to ourselves to learn how to recognize behaviors that reflect and escalate anxiety—and to manage our own anxiety so it doesn't get played out in hurtful ways."

The Rival

Our jealousy meter goes up or down depending on how much threat we assess that a rival poses to our relationship. First, we check her out on a scale of comparative attributes: Hers vs. Mine. Not all rivals are created equal. Whether we're male or female, we experience more jealousy when our rival appears to surpass our attractiveness or achievements. Women tend to size up their rival (real or perceived) as either a tough competitor or no threat depending on her looks and charm. Men's jealousy tends to rise and fall depending on whether or not they think their rival (real or perceived) is more or less of an alpha male than they are.

Guarding Your Mate

Jealousy in its mildest form is your wake-up call to pay more attention to your partner. The root of jealousy is a retro-emotion arising from the dark but outmoded logic of our DNA. It is an alarm system to warn you that someone harbors the evil intention of stealing your mate. Over time we have evolved and learned how to rein in our ancient and overzealous instincts so we can function in our coed modern world, but our inner cavewoman lingers. To our credit, we have developed clever ways to signal that our mate is off-limits without hitting a rival over the head with a mallet. Nando Pelusi, a psychologist in private practice in New York City, gives us clues to spotting such ploys: "The most basic strategy is mate-guarding, on display during any cocktail party or Sunday stroll through the park: the innocent urge to put your arm around your partner in a casual conversation; the not-so-innocent mention of a partner's flaws, as if to say, 'Trust me, this person is not the dazzling package she appears to be.' These are time-honored techniques to fend off potential rivals." In that kind of sexy interplay, one colored with a sly overture of possessiveness, "mate guarding" isn't harmful; it is jealousy lite. Actually, your feminine gesture of mentally tattooing your name on his arm can be useful. It reminds you that there is a lot of competition out there and can move you to shape up both your appearance and your appreciation of him as your adored mate.

A Suspicious Mind

Beyond the occasional times when you catch a mild case of the jealous flu, you need to be aware of how jealousy can turn into a serious illness. Jealousy feeds on itself by constantly nipping away at our insecurity with imagined scenarios of personal betrayal. And a bad case of jealousy manifests itself by making us overly vigilant about everything our partner might be thinking, and most important, doing. Women have been known to do wacky (even illegal) things, like googling his ex-girlfriend or ex-wife and sending her a "stay away from my man" e-mail, stalking him to see what he is up to, checking his phone bills and making anonymous calls to the unfamiliar numbers or ones he frequently calls, writing down the mileage on his car and keeping a log of his trips, hiring a technician to hack into his computer—the list goes on and on. (More than a few women I interviewed confided in me that they have done one or more of the above. I know I have.)

Elvis Presley's great recording "Suspicious Minds" is a textbook of how a woman's bottomless pit of insecurity about her partner being sexually true blue sets into motion a backlash from him. Our suspicious fears that he will abandon us can become a self-fulfilling prophecy. It has been proven that excessive and obsessive jealousy doesn't make your partner cuddle up and want to stay close to home. Instead it drives the partner who is under constant surveillance away, usually into the arms of another lover, which ironically convinces the jealous person that she was right in the first place.

The Other Woman

If in any form of grim reality your jealous nightmares do materialize and your partner leaves you, the aftermath of jealousy can take a menacing and ugly turn, one manifested in fury and anger at being cast aside for another woman. As the universal cliché goes: "There is no fury like a woman scorned." There is, sadly, some truth there. If another woman is identified as "the other woman," it isn't unusual for us to be as angry and furious at her for "stealing" our "irreplaceable" man as we are at him for straying. Plots of revenge are written and rewritten and often acted out: eggs thrown at windows, air let out of tires, phone calls at all hours of the day (at work) and night (at his place or hers). At the extreme end of the unleashed vengeance of a woman scorned is the image most of us can still call up on instant replay—the grisly scene from the movie *Fatal Attraction* when the camera zoomed in on a bunny boiling in a pot. Bunnies aside, at its most destructive mode jealousy is not a rare motive for homicide (though it tends to be a motive of men more than women).

Games Jealousy Plays

We have been led to believe that an absence of jealousy may be a sign that your lover is lukewarm or doesn't share the same depth of passion that you feel. Unfortunately, in an attempt to stoke those fires, women are much more likely than men to deliberately try to make their partners jealous. Women tend to play-act both subtle and outrageous dramas to induce jealousy in their lovers—usually by flirting, dressing provocatively to get men's attention, and sometimes going so far as to date another guy. Are our cunning "make him jealous" strategies a test of the relationship? (Are you serious about me?) Or are they an attempt to gain more romantic attention and commitment from him? (I might fall for someone else if you don't step up to the plate.) The problem is that a woman often thinks her man will respond the way she does when she feels jealous or threatened. That is, he will make a greater effort to court her and build a cozier nest for two. She has overlooked one significant detail: typically men don't react that way. Men tend to feel humiliated and "played" when subjected to this ploy. You may only succeed in gaining the opportunity to wave good-bye as he sprints out the door to find a woman who "appreciates" and "trusts" him. As Stan, a computer programmer from Cleveland, explains: "A woman may think coming on to other guys will make a guy hot and bothered and shape up to please her, but all it does is give him permission to get drunk and 'get screwed.' "

Raising the Red Flag

Deeply felt and acted-out jealousy is often referred to as a "crime of passion," but that is so off-base. It has nothing to do with authentic passion. At its extreme, jealousy is about rage, vengeance, and self-loathing. Pay close attention when a partner, or a potential partner, shows any amount of jealousy that upsets you or displays a pattern of getting hot under the collar using the excuse that "he is jealous." What clouds our judgment about how to handle the situation is that jealousy is glamorized in romantic novels and in the sex-betrayal sagas we see in never-ending soap-opera-genre TV shows and movies. It is too easy to fall into the trap of believing that his behavior reflects his undying passion for you. It doesn't. It is a yellow flag warning you to slow down and pay attention to the conditions of the road ahead. Without delay, together you need to consult a counselor and find out what is at the root of the behavior. But if at any time your partner threatens you physically, or actually shoves, slaps, or hits you, you have just witnessed a red flag unfolding. It is a clear and dangerous signal that the time has come to put Gus on the Bus or, according to the blues group Little Charlie and the Nightcats, "Dump the Chump"—whatever; you pack up and leave. Don't make excuses for him; this kind of behavior is never acceptable and rarely changes.

Coping with the Temptations of Jealousy

Most people agree that as adults we can and should exercise control over our emotions (witness the popularity of "anger management" courses). Strangely, jealousy—maybe because it is all about sex and ego—usually gets a free pass. In my seminars, people sincerely say that they don't believe you can control being jealous. Either you are the jealous type or you aren't. It turns out to sound right, but it is all wrong. Don't allow yourself to slip into the facile assumption that because your emotions are derived from a woolly mixture of genes, neurotransmitters, hormones, and upbringing your emotions are beyond your control. You can stifle your jealous reactions and emotions by deciding not to be jealous. Yes, it is that simple. It takes a conscious decision on your part not to allow jealousy to be a part of who you are and not to allow it to be the uninvited guest in your passionate relationship. Granted, your emotions derive from a complex dance of brain and body, but jealousy is malleable; you can control your green-eyed monster more than it can control you.

Don't get caught up in the romanticized notion that your partner's jealousy is a compliment. It may be a sign that he is immature and insecure or a clue that you (and he) need to address problems in your relationship. Deal with what is behind his jealous feelings, not what the sappy media would lead you to believe is a sign of true love. In truth, when jealousy begins to seep into the picture, conflict and discord are not far behind.

The most effective antidote to the poison of jealousy is envisioning yourself as a whole person, with or without him. The first positive step is to put away fears of being dumped for another woman—abandoned to become a bitter woman with twelve cats living in a smelly apartment. Or whatever the negative anxiety attacks are that feed into your obsession about losing him. Don't allow yourself to be sucked into the quicksand of dependence, believing you will wither away without him. What helps the most is to tune in to yourself: the woman who laughs, goes barefoot, dishes with the girls, and does a mean Christina Aguilera while driving down the highway—a person who values being passionately in love but can go it alone until she finds it.

9

Our Cheating Hearts

Breaking Down
the Walls of Secrecy

Why do couples break up? Bitter quarrels, insensitive remarks, too little sex, too much unsatisfying sex, jam on the butter knife, money problems—the reasons men or women give for why they leave are as varied as their motives for having gotten into the relationship in the first place. Yet of all the reasons people give for being torn apart, getting angry to the bone, and then putting one foot out the door, overt infidelity heads the list.

I can't wave a magic wand over you to ensure that each of you will be sexually faithful to each other forever. I can, however, offer you background on the dynamics of affairs to help kick-start a conversation on the topic between you and the man in your life (either in a budding or a long-term relationship), along with some practical advice about how to keep a passionate love between you and your partner grounded.

The Love Affair?
The Lust Affair?

In the movie *City Slickers*, when Billy Crystal's character is asked about being tempted to cheat, he says that the question doesn't relate to him because, as he puts it, "I'm married. I caught my legal limit." How do you feel about monogamy, adultery, afternoon delights, extramarital relationships, two-timing, cheating, and infidelity? I'm not asking about semantics here but about how you really feel about being sexually exclusive and taking vows of commitment to "forsake all others." Do you believe that vows of monogamy are a nonissue or just plain nonsense? If you believe a passionate relationship means being sexually exclusive, how ready and able are you to be true to your beliefs? Yet another tough question: any idea how your partner feels about all of the above?

Take, for instance, how authors Cathi Hanauer and Dan Jones struggled over the issue of marriage and fidelity. Before their wedding, she had her doubts about marriage and the vows of fidelity. "I wasn't sure I could handle it," she said. "I was ambivalent about monogamy and worried that I could not remain faithful to one person for the rest of my life.

"I wanted to add to my vows the words 'I'll try very hard,' but Dan wouldn't go for it."

Cathi, in her disarmingly honest way, put into words what so many people don't have the courage to discuss before vowing to "forsake all others."

Whether you discuss it or not, the possibility that you or your partner could fall into lust with someone else—in fantasies or otherwise—shadows every passionate relationship. The unvarnished truth is that sexual affairs happen in good relationships just as often as in bad ones. And the stark facts about fidelity are twofold: *You can't make another person be sexually faithful. And you alone are responsible for your own fidelity to your partner.*

Swimming Through Muddy Waters

What muddies the water in describing cheating is that we are used to thinking about illicit sexual relationships in the context of marriage—where at least one party is married. But that definition doesn't work any more in our living-together world. Our understanding of the meaning of "cheating" has changed over the decades. Consider that it was once called fornication and cited in the dictionary as sexual relations between an unmarried woman and a married man (no sexism there!). Now it is defined as "consensual sexual intercourse between two persons not married to each other." Adultery—the sexual unfaithfulness of a married person, once widely publicly condemned—is now a word and an action decried mostly in church sermons as a sin, a major betrayal of family values, and a righteous reason for divorce. Outside of those arenas, you don't hear much talk of "adultery" anymore.

To ensure that we are on the same page, when I say *affair* or *having an affair* or *cheating* or *infidelity* I am referring to when a person who is in a committed relationship—not only marriage—is having a secret sexual relationship outside of that committed relationship. When I refer to a person involved in a secret, sexual relationship I use the words *unfaithful partner* when in a good mood and *the betrayer* when in a less forgiving mood.

There is a paradox about how we feel vs. how we act about cheating. While polls indicate 90 percent of the respondents disapprove of cheating, surveys reveal that infidelity is not a rare bird. The National Opinion Research Center at the University of Chicago found that 15 percent of wives and 25 percent of husbands have had an affair. Other research, usually found in popular magazines and online, tend to inflate the numbers—some report that 40 to 60 percent of married people admit having cheated on their mates at least once. There isn't really any scientific way to know how many people have sex with another person outside of their committed relationships. People lie to their partners, and people lie to survey takers.

Moving on to make the point that sexual cheating is much more common than our society owns up to, we turn to modern medical science and DNA testing. In a recent study, when newborn children and their parents were tested, about 15 percent of the babies were found not to be related to the mothers' husbands. Go figure.

Despite the distressing statistics about the prevalence of cheating, the numbers don't give us a true picture of fidelity. Vast numbers of couples practice serial monogamy and are sexually excusive in each relationship. And many couples are sexually faithful over a lifetime of being together.

The Walls of Secrecy, Lies, and Deception

Infidelity isn't only about sex; it is more about secrecy, deception, and lying. And when people tell lies about seri-

ous matters, they tell them more to their romantic partners than to anyone else. Can you tell when your partner is
lying? Unless you are very tuned in to him, it's not likely.
When we are intimate, we have a bias toward truth that
leads us to assume that our partner is being honest with us.
Ironically, the more intimate we become, the less capable we
are of detecting deception.

Lies, despite how common they are, have a poisonous
effect on a passionate relationship. Liars know they are lying
and in most cases are wary of being found out. They build
a wall of secrecy around themselves, cover their tracks, and
are on constant guard to avoid discovery. Thus, the cover-up
itself becomes a wedge between the two partners in a committed partnership. As author Scott Peck warned us, "Bear
in mind that the act of withholding the truth is always
potentially a lie and that in each instance in which the truth
is withheld a significant moral decision is required."

Breaking the Codes

You might think that "sexual exclusivity" and "being sexually faithful" are pretty clear concepts. Not so. It turns outs
out that most of us have our own private code of sexually
faithful behavior, and most of us never discuss it with our
partner. A sampling of these codes might include "Cheat on
me and you are gone," "You can look, but don't touch," and
"Don't ask, don't tell." The problem is that you may think
the code is "Do it in secret and don't fall in love" while
your partner thinks the mutually agreed-on code is "We are
a sexually monogamous couple." Complicating this issue
even more is that there is wide disagreement about what

exactly defines "having sex"—from President Clinton saying "I didn't have sex with that woman" to high school girls today saying giving a guy a blow job isn't "sex" to Jessie, a twenty-nine-year-old photographer who tells me as long as she doesn't allow her lover to "go all the way" she is having an affair but isn't cheating on her husband.

It is important to be clear about how each of you defines "having sex" and what constitutes "cheating." A relationship with miscues and ambiguity about monogamy is a tricky kind of commitment. In any case, a passionate relationship requires that each partner know the code and agree to the code.

Why Do We Stray?

One aspect of cheating is without question: infidelity brings heartbreak in its wake because we've been taught to pretend it doesn't exist or will "never happen to us." It would be foolish or naive to believe that you or your partner will never be tempted to have an affair. In truth, being in love with someone does not prevent us from being in lust with someone else. Some people act on those lustful feelings; some don't.

Those who sexually cheat on their mates are usually considered to be morally weak, selfish, two-timing jerks. Undeniably, some are all of that and more. Others are stand-up folks except in a situation where they lack the guts to tell their partners that it is over between them and that they want out. Others simply want to have their cake and eat it too.

Since infidelity is such a heart-wounding issue, you would be wise to gain a greater understanding of why people might sexually cheat on their mates even if you think you will never have any use for the information. As the sports world puts it, "The best defense is a good offense." So let's take a step back and review the most common scenarios (or excuses) of why people get caught up in an affair.

It Just Happens

Having an affair is not generally planned; emotions sometimes just drift from friendship into sexual desire and from there into sex. Usually the two people involved know each other from working and/or socializing together. It's much rarer, but cheating also "happens" with a stranger—one thing leads to another, and before you know it it's dawn and there he is in the same bed with you.

There is no greater myth than "it just happened." It may have not been planned with spreadsheets and timelines, but nothing *just happens*. We make it happen. Or we don't. People who say they didn't plan for sex to happen either are in denial or have lousy memories.

A Player Personality

People who have frequent and multiple affairs tend to be unable (or unwilling) to empathize with the feelings of the people they are having sex with and with all those who might be impacted negatively by their sexual behaviors, such as their mate (if they have one), children, the mates of others, friends, and colleagues. Up through the late 1960s, the

"Free Love" movement was glorified and a sexual revolution was in the air. But now the widespread AIDS epidemic has singlehandedly inspired the "Safe Sex" movement, putting a damper on casual sex. Players are still out there, though, and they ought to wear a P-embroidered shroud as a warning because they are smooth actors and very seductive lovers. Be aware that players often use a "decoy fib" to cover up that they are living with someone, such as "I'm in the process of getting the wrinkles out of the divorce [or separation]" or "My girlfriend is moving out as soon as she can find a place." Mostly they are sex addicts and will never be satisfied with one lover. If a man you are interested in or the man in your life has a history of cheating, you need to know that unless he has gone through counseling about ending his cheating ways, he is very likely to be a repeat offender.

Romance Interrupted

The situation here involves people who say that because they are unfulfilled in their primary relationship they yearn to experience the deep bond of romantic love. There is a fine line here between those who say they are seeking an outside relationship to fill the gap in their emotional or sexual needs and those who are caught up in an unrealistic search for the perfect mate—the "He Walks on Water" fantasy guy. Irrespective of those who are given over to old-fashioned lust or romantic fantasies, some folks in this group may be genuinely love-hungry souls yearning for a heart connection.

More often than not, the romantic affair lover will turn out to have feet of clay and the affair will crumble. But if the lovers decide they can't live without each other, a split or a divorce will soon be in the works for the original couples, which leads to a mess all around.

We don't really know how many couples start out in a clandestine affair and then become legitimate partners. You have to wonder if they will live happily ever after this time around. Trust has got to be an issue.

Lust Unfilled

These are the people who say they are purely motivated by the pleasure of having sex with someone other than their mate. They say that having sex with the same person gets boring after a while and enjoying sex with someone new reignites their sexual desires. Some believe that having an affair outside of their primary relationship (most often a married relationship) benefits not only them but their mates as well, because they insist that they bring home a rejuvenated interest in sex and are better lovers. These unfaithful folks feed off an endless supply of self-deception.

My DNA Made Me Do It

Although scientists disagree about the role genetics play in sexual cheating, the scales tip in favor of the point of view that as human beings we are not programmed for a lifetime of monogamy. Sexual affairs in some form or another appear in every culture and have since time before time. Lifetime "pair bonding" isn't as programmed into the human species as it is in swans, which are said to mate for life. (Actually, recent studies are now less certain abut swans.) Some researchers, anthropologists for example, contend that having more than one lover is the way of our flesh. According to that view, we are programmed to be nonmonogamous to increase the chances of our species' genes surviving into the next generation.

Despite the pull of our randy genes and our philandering history, most people make a conscious effort to be faithful to their partner as long as they are together. (*Note*: An old study about menstrual cycles and sexual desire found that while there was no pattern to when women had sex with their steady partners, having sex on the side peaked at the height of women's fertility cycles. It would be interesting to see what a current study might reveal.)

The Circes of Cyberspace

The Internet has become the new frontier for those who are tempted to stray. Despite the lack of physical contact, emotional Internet relationships aren't necessarily benign relationships, because most of them contain one or more elements that spell trouble ahead for a committed relationship: (1) the emotional intensity of the Internet relationship often comes at the expense of the committed relationship's emotional connection, (2) the deception builds a wall of secrecy between the real-life partners, and (3) there is an underlying sexual chemistry between I-lovers that doesn't get dampened by the monotonous details of sharing a daily (and real) life.

In these Internet emotional connections, there is often the temptation to take it up a notch—to meet in person and (I'm shocked!) have sex. In which case, the Internet relationship officially crosses the line from finding a kindred spirit to cheating.

Out of Town or Under the Influence or Both

In this scenario, we have people who say they have affairs only when they are out of town and therefore it doesn't count. They may feel guilty, but not enough to stop doing it. Others say they got drunk or were on drugs and don't recall how they ended up having sex. Whatever excuse is used to explain away this behavior, it doesn't hold water. (See the "It Just Happens" scenario above.)

The Lure of the Spider Woman

Kevin, a man attending a workshop in Louisville, describes a woman who pursues a married man as a "spider woman." Because, he says, "She sucks blood from you and then leaves you to die or with overwhelming guilt and shame that you cheated on your wife for a worthless affair." The voice of experience?

I've always wondered how a woman who has an affair with a man she knows with certainty is in a relationship with another woman could possibly kid herself that he will be faithful to her. I've heard too many weepy stories told by women devastated because "he" cheated on her. It is hard to offer a shoulder to cry on and a clean handkerchief when you find out that she knew he had a woman at home waiting for him while she, our tearful betrayed woman, was heating up the bed sheets with him.

It's not only a mistake to have an affair with a married man or a man in a committed relationship; it is a mistake to think he will ever leave his wife or his partner. Recall the scene in the movie *When Harry Met Sally* (if not, rent it) where the Carrie Fisher character is having lunch with her girlfriends (one being Meg Ryan). She laments that "he" will never leave his wife for the millionth time, and her girlfriends respond like a weary Greek chorus in agreement: *"He will never leave her."* Even if the unfaithful guy does divorce his wife, it is unlikely that he will end up marrying the "other woman." Given the stories I've heard from both men and women, a good number of such men end up marrying someone else.

Each of us is responsible for our own good and bad behavior, including Kevin, our Louisville guy with the take on spider women. No one can "steal" anyone from anyone, not even the cunning spider woman. But what happened to the sisterhood pledge that if a man is in a committed relationship he is off-limits? That time-honored tradition of hooking our little fingers to seal the deal that he is "hers" has saved many a broken heart. Elizabeth Rae Larson, a therapist with the Seattle Institute for Sex Therapy, Education and Research, offers us good advice: "Do not have a sexual affair with a married man unless he brings a note from his wife."

Facing Realities About a Nonmonogamous Man

If a man tells you he is uncertain about making a commitment to be sexually exclusive, believe him. He is giving you an honest response. You may not like what he says, but accept that he is, at least, not hiding behind a cowardly lie.

If a man tells you he has never been monogamous in the past, don't kid yourself that you have the magical power to change him because he says he intends to be monogamous with you. He might change and become a true-blue sexually faithful partner, but until he has proven that he is sexually faithful for at least a year, consider him nonmonogamous. Melissa's story isn't the usual "cheating" story, but it offers insight into how many of us really feel about "man sharing." Mostly, it sheds light on how easy it is to get caught up with love and infidelity.

Melissa, an attractive woman in her thirties and owner of a successful trendy café, confided in me the details of a relationship that caught her off guard. After two years of grieving over a failed marriage she met Kyle, an architect in his late forties, at a book club she had joined to meet new people. She says, "He was charming, witty, and the guy all the single women swooned over. It was an instant attraction. We went out to lunch two days later and hit it off immediately. A few days later he invited me up to his place for homemade pizza. He had a wonderful condo, full of books and art. I was thrilled to find a man I had so much in common with. But over coffee he got quiet, took my hand in his, and told me that he had to be absolutely honest with me if we planned to continue seeing each other. He said he wasn't a monogamous man and had several women in his life that he loved and saw as much as possible. One lived in the same town we did, and the others lived in other parts of the States and in Europe. I was, to be honest, inwardly crushed. Outwardly, I just put on a happy face and said that I wasn't looking for a serious relationship and I enjoyed my freedom as well. One big fat lie.

Over the next six months we saw each other several times a week and spoke more than once a day by phone. He never mentioned the monogamy thing again, and I saw no evidence that he was involved with anyone else (and I did look). That all changed when he told me he was leaving in two weeks for a month in Mexico with Tamara, a woman he had been in a relationship for over five years and who lived in London. I was disappointed, but again I put on my happy face—my "independent woman" mask.

Over the next two years we had a wonderful relationship except when he left town to see the other women in his life. His need to have other women was deeply troubling to me, but I was enjoying having a man in my life again, and I swear I thought I saw signs that he was beginning to reevaluate being sexually faithful. The shit hit the fan when he announced that Tamara was coming in a few weeks to spend a month with him and it would be better if we did not see each other while she was here. He assured me she knew all about me, but it would be uncomfortable for everyone. My entire sophisticated pretense about how I felt about monogamy shattered. After the first week of sheer hell knowing she was sleeping in the same bed I had shared with him, I got "out of Dodge" to save my sanity and my dignity. It took me a few more months to face up to the reality that he would never be a one-woman man. Call me old-fashioned, but I want the man I'm with to be with only me and me to be only with him. I've seen Kyle from time to time out with different women, and we are cordial. I shake my head in disbelief that I thought he was a leopard whose spots I could change. Thank God, I met a terrific man a few months ago, and we agree about being sexually exclusive—it isn't an issue at all."

Like Melissa, it is too easy to fall into the belief that we can sprinkle faithful dust on a man to make him into a sexually exclusive partner. Be aware that you are more susceptible when a better man isn't on the horizon or when you have just come out of a relationship that didn't work out. Having a man in your life who makes you unhappy about sexual fidelity is more lonely and damaging to your self-esteem than not having a man in your life.

Adding Up the Price of Cheating

Whether a relationship is three weeks old or three years old, the consequences of cheating are similar. True, we no longer stone, flog, or put a woman who commits adultery into the stocks to brand her as a wanton whore. There are no more scarlet letters. Yet, there is no such thing as a "free" affair—not for you, not for the man in your life. This much is for sure: the discovery of an affair evokes different types of responses and reactions on the part of the betrayed, some predictable, some not.

Most of us would be far less likely to become involved in an affair if we first considered what is at stake. And that depends on a lot of different things, such as whether a couple has children, whether they are part of a tight group of family and friends, whether the affair seemed to come out of the blue, and so forth. Putting any differences aside, here is a brief and sad rundown of the most common consequences of cheating:

- Trust is the foundation of every passionate relationship. When cheating is discovered, the betrayed partner has to rework his or her entire perception of the other person and their relationship. Once trust has been broken, it is very difficult to put it back together. Finding out your partner has been unfaithful is a direct hit to the heart. One woman told me she felt she was being sucked into an emotional undertow of every bad movie of the "other woman" she had seen when she found out her partner was having an affair. Although that was five years ago (followed by a divorce four years ago), she says, "I can still feel the despair and pain. It has dulled with time, but it went deep."

- Friends tend to take sides with the "innocent party" when an affair is revealed. Those who have relationship problems of their own will feel very threatened and end the friendship with the wayward person. Friends have also been known to drop both the "innocent party" and "the noninnocent party" because having to tiptoe around the debris of a wrecked relationship makes them uncomfortable.

- Folk wisdom is easy to remember because it makes sense, such as "The grass is always greener on the other side of the fence." An attractive guy could be very appealing from what you can see from your side of the fence, but once you jump over the fence the grass might not look so emerald green and lush. Usually, looking back over to the side you were on—the one with a loving, committed partner—looks pretty good, if not better than the new turf. But after jumping over the fence you may not be welcomed back to the side from whence you came.

Is It Cheating If It Happens Only in My Head?

A question I often get in seminars runs along these lines: is fantasizing about having an affair with a person you know or with a person you don't know, say a famous person, "cheating"? The answer is no. Sexual thoughts and fantasies are just that—the spinning of sensual desires played out in the imagination. If you're fantasizing while having sex that your partner is the hunky cable repair man that showed up to restore your cable reception last week, does that mean you no longer passionately love your guy? No— hot thoughts aren't the same thing as hot actions; they are only sweet or spicy candy for the mind.

As Rachel, a nurse practitioner, explains, "Just because I'm married and have stopped looking for a partner doesn't mean that I've gone lust dead! When I see a sexy man, I wonder what he would be like in bed. Sometimes I see a man that is the opposite physical type of my partner and wonder if he is a good kisser, a good lover. I wonder how I would feel having sex with a differently shaped body and with a differently shaped penis. It gives me a sexy thrill. I think if you don't have sexual fantasies, you aren't alive. Once you stop looking, you get old."

It is harmless to fantasize about romance and sex with other men. At the same time, it usually isn't wise to share all of your fantasies with your partner. There is no reason to—your fantasies are yours to savor— but if you really want to do so, use tact and caution. On one hand, sharing could increase candor and intimacy. On the other, it could freak out your partner to learn what goes on in that wild-woman mind of yours. You be the judge.

The Irony of It All

The irony is that most affairs consist of hot and horny e-mails, cutesy text messages, breathy phone messages, and a lot of lousy sex after the initial thrill is gone. Reflecting on an affair that blew up in their faces, most people say living a life of deception was sheer hell and the heartbreak they caused their partners wasn't worth it.

Keep the Wolf of Temptation Away from Your Door

Despite our nonmonogamist nature, we aren't robots programmed to cheat. We have brains that equip us with the insight necessary for foresight, the gift of language and spatial perception, and other wonderful abilities that we can use to keep any proclivity for being unfaithful under control. Specifically, you can create an environment in your relationship that makes it less likely that either of you will stray.

Stoke the Fires of Passion

Apathy and neglect are the two biggest killers of what was once a happy, passionate relationship. Whether it is through acting out your sexual fantasies and the lavish bestowal of teddies and garter-belted black stockings on your mate or lost weekends in hotels or erotic toys, you—as a passionate and imaginative lover—are sure to be able to generate the sense of novelty our primitive hearts desire within (not outside of) your committed relationships.

Steer Him Out of Harm's Way

It is good to know that when you are passionately in love you have a built-in safeguard mechanism that instinctively responds to signs that the man in your life may be vulnerable to falling through temptation's trapdoor. It is that gut feeling you get when your mate appears to be a bit too interested in another woman, a sense you get either by observing him at a social gathering or by noticing that he's bringing up her name in conversation for no good reason. Or maybe it's *her* intense interest you notice, and it doesn't look like she is trolling for a platonic friendship. Usually he looks oh-so-unaware of the dynamics involved. Maybe he is; maybe he is enjoying the attention.

Your uneasiness isn't going to be alleviated by your becoming a jealous hag or getting into an argument about his (or her) intentions. Those behaviors make you look ridiculous and insecure and make him or her look like a saint. The best way to avoid trouble is to gently lead him away from temptation.

A few weeks ago, for instance, I became engaged in a spirited (read: flirty) conversation with a very attractive man at an art gallery opening about a painting he professed to love and I didn't. Suddenly I felt the whooshes of her skirt as his "significant other" appeared like magic, hooked her arm into his, and began to steer him in the direction of the other end of the gallery because he had to see a "wonderful landscape." She managed to give me a subtle "Don't even think about it, sister!" look once I was out of his line of sight. I really chuckled and wanted to give her an "Atta Girl" high five. She made all the right moves and did it with style and grace.

Keep the Windows of Intimacy Wide Open

Stay connected on the same wavelength by talking and listening to each other. A relationship between you and your partner precludes either of you being a "silent partner." There must be ongoing, regular talking and listening about both worries and upbeat news for your relationship to maintain the passion between you. To paraphrase Stephen Covey's famous advice: "Seek first to understand and then to be understood." Each person has to feel he or she is truly heard and valued. Saying "I love you" with passion and sincerity is music to your partner's ears.

To Err Is Human; to Forgive, Divine

Telling your partner how miserable you would be if he were ever to be unfaithful is less effective than telling him what you want—sexual exclusivity. Even more effective is keeping a positive vision that you both will be sexually faithful. There is a caveat here. Being straightforward about how each of you feels about this issue is certainly worthy of discussing, but it is foolish to throw down the gauntlet and declare that infidelity is nonnegotiable grounds for a breakup unless you really mean it. In other words, don't make pronouncements you will regret later.

Relationships are complex and worthy of more than a sermonlike judgment call that the only action you would take if he were unfaithful would be to kick him to the curb. You can't be certain how you might react to his being unfaithful. Put another way: you can't really project what action you might take about an action he might take until he takes it.

Leslie, a woman who stayed after one of my seminars, tells me she has a question for me but first wants to give me some background. "I always knew if Gary [her husband] cheated on me, he would be out the door. Things were fine, but after we had been together for three years, we had to deal with some very difficult financial issues. He was downsized out of his job and had to work out of state for about eight months. During that time he confessed that he had had an affair. Actually, I accused him of it, because after I returned home from visiting him, I had a funny feeling something didn't feel right. After he confessed, I did think of leaving him. But he is really remorseful and has not placed the blame on anyone but himself. After counseling and a lot of soul searching, we are slowly putting our relationship back on track. I still love him, but the trust is still not there—it's getting better, but not there yet. I confided in two of my closest girlfriends, and their reactions were so negative. All I got from them was 'Once a cheat, always a cheat' and that I should 'send him packing.' It is very discouraging. My question for you is: do you think that we can mend our relationship, or am I setting myself up for heartache?"

First, I congratulated Leslie on her and her husband's efforts to keep the relationship going by tackling the problem as one they have to work on together. Then I encouraged her to stop seeking advice from anyone but a counselor. Girlfriends can help us over most of the bumps on the relationship road, but the issue of sexual cheating—when it is you or him—is so volatile that it is best to keep what happened in your relationship confidential. Our girlfriends are honor-bound to side with us against the cheating partner, which works against reconciliation.

Infidelity brings heartbreak in its wake because we've been taught to pretend it doesn't exist or will "never happen to us." I wonder if cheating might lose its power to shock and devastate us if we were better prepared for at least the possibility that one or both of use could stray from the nest.

Still, minus a crystal ball none of us can predict how a relationship will survive the revelation of an affair. But for the record, forgiveness and moving beyond the infidelity are much more likely to happen in close, intimate, and committed relationships than those that aren't committed. Many couples not only survive the affair, but their relationships grow stronger and more intimate. It seems that when you and your partner are more acutely tuned in to what each of you needs to feel satisfied—both emotionally and sexually— you are freed to be more passionate lovers.

Cheating Isn't Inevitable

As I've said, take heart. The true story behind the overblown headlines claiming that infidelity is the new American pastime is that most of us are faithful to our lovers—serially, one at a time—or with one lover over a lifetime.

10

The Chilling of Desire

Clearly, I'm dedicated to helping you make a passionate love work. Nevertheless, I am a realist. I recognize that most relationships, no matter how promising they are at the beginning, won't develop into a deeply loving and sensual partnership.

In this chapter, you'll find advice about how to recognize and deal with a change of heart—yours or his—and how to accept love's demise by exiting gracefully and being generous and compassionate. Because most relationships are destined to end, it is important to learn no-blame and no-fault ways to navigate through love's stormy weather without anyone's heart getting broken beyond repair. Ending a relationship in a kind and caring way isn't only taking the high ground (which is, by itself, good for the soul—civility trumps acrimony); it also allows you to fall in love again minus the baggage of anger or disappointment over a relationship that didn't last.

Where Did the Love Go?

What are the underlying dynamics of the unraveling of the romantic and sexual ties between couples? There isn't one universal break-up story that sheds light on why love fades away or ends abruptly or why one partner falls out of love and the other partner continues to be in love. There are as many reasons why people fall out of love as there are reasons why they fall in love. However, studies do show that prematurely expecting any outcome, from abandonment to marriage, tends to make some people step on either the brakes or the accelerator, even though the relationship is still in a formative stage.

I've never forgotten a snippet from a short story I read about the ending of a romance. It seems the narrator knew the *exact* moment it was over for him: when he looked up from his book and watched his lover reach over the coffee table to answer the phone. Just like that. Can love hang by such a slender thread? Apparently, it can, at least for some of us.

Love's passions faded away for some lovers because they say that their loving feelings eroded over one argument at a time. Others say they knew that one day their turbulent relationship would finally end in a high-drama uproar, followed by an explosive and satisfying door-slamming exit. And for other lovers, once the highly anticipated ring of the phone that set their hearts on fire becomes a too familiar ring, once the high trapeze act of "falling in love" is replaced by cozy warmth of "being in love," their relationship takes a downshift and eventually ends.

Even though people say they can remember the exact point at which they fell out of love, the demise of love is, in fact, rarely sudden. Love is blind only to the extent that it conceals the number of arrows your lover has shot into your heart—or when you are the archer, the number of arrows you have aimed at him. Feeling that you share a special love enables you to endure those misplaced arrows—such as lack of affection and attention or blowups or boorishness—up to a point.

Once a crucial threshold is reached, there may be no going back. In many cases, a love that is repeatedly wounded never regains its strength. No amount of apologies, tears, and promises to play nicer may be enough to recreate the emotions of being in love again.

Why Relationships Don't Gell

It is difficult to determine exactly why a promising relationship doesn't measure up to its promise. While circumstances vary, there appear to be similar underlying causes. The timing for a serious romance is off—a new job, just broke up, moving to a new city, working on a college degree, elderly parents need care, and so forth. Maybe one of the lovers doesn't have a burning desire to hitch his or her wagon to anyone's star and would rather keep all options open. Or the issue could be in the very nature of passion itself. As psychologist Elaine Hartfield observed, "Passionate love is kindled by a sprinkle of hope and a large dollop of loneliness, mourning, jealousy and terror." Thus, it could be that for some people, when faced with the emotions generated by passionate love, swim away for fear of getting caught in the undertow.

Some people may crave intimacy but at the same time not know how to handle it; they sabotage a relationship as soon as closeness develops. Other lovers, sensing even the slightest hint that the relationship may be in danger, start displaying distancing behavior and prepare an escape route if the alarm goes off. Lovers who anticipate rejection may reject first, like quitting a job before they think they will be fired. And, then there are the lovers who, when things get messy or chaotic—even though their love feelings are still strong—leave because they want a "no-hassles" relationship. For instance, Jack Berger, Carrie's angst-ridden boyfriend in "Sex and the City," sneaked out the door as she slept, leaving a break-up Post-it note on her computer. A memorable moment.

Being the First to Say Good-Bye

When it becomes undeniable that your relationship will never work, in the hope of making a nimble retreat you are likely to avail yourself of the classic exit excuse: "It's not you; it's me." It is a time-honored way to walk away with dignity. But ask yourself: Are you simply being honest with your lover that your feelings changed and you want to step up to the plate and take responsibility? Are you assuming the blame for the ending of a relationship as a sneaky way to avoid a dramatic scene? Or are you offering a way to help your lover save face because you still love him, even though you no longer are *in* love with him?

In fact, unless he is guilty of abuse, neglect or deceit, he may have had little influence on your changing passionate emotions. There are many needs and desires that connect you to your partner, and as your love needs and desires change, the timbre of your love changes. Your relationship may get stronger, or it may get weaker. If it's the latter, discontent is not far behind.

Whatever your reasons are for wanting to end it, you need be honest with yourself to gain a deeper understanding of what has brought you to this turning point in your love life. Are you tired of making endless compromises in order to sustain it? Is it that you love him, but not enough to make either one of you happy in the long run? Or do you hear the tick tock of the bio-clock and feel you can't waste any more time in a relationship that is good but not great? Giving considerable thought about why this relationship didn't jell for you is invaluable in helping you make the next relationship—the one you have always wanted—work.

There Is No Easy Way Out

Being the one who takes the initiative to end the relationship won't get you a get-out-of-jail-for-free card. Despite how tactful you are and how rational and righteous your reasons are, a break-up is a rough emotional ride. Although you can feel deeply distraught over the love's ending, don't feel guilty and disloyal because it is over for you but not for him. Don't make things worse by prolonging the inevitable.

When He Says Those Fatal Words

When your heart is firmly pinned on your sleeve, it is hard to hear the words "It's over" coming from the lips of the man you love—and harder yet to accept them. It feels like a dagger to the heart. You can't avoid the pain, but you can lessen it by resigning yourself to the reality that it is doubtful you can change his mind. Yes, miracles happen, but rarely.

Resist the temptation to act on the need for a prolonged "closure." Rip up that "why he sucks" list you keep hidden in the hip pocket of your mind itemizing his faults. Most of us can haul out a laundry list of grievances: his sloppy habits, his overbearing mother, his lack of attention to what you are interested in, his credit-card balances, and so on and on. (*Note*: we rarely make a list of how we might have contributed to the relationship falling apart.) But letting "it" (humiliation, rejection, astonishment, feelings of betrayal) all hang out won't change a thing. It won't make you or him feel one iota better or insure fond memories of the way you were.

Comedian Bob Ettinger gives us some light-hearted "rules" that should govern an ex-lover's exit: "Being in a relationship is like a full-time job, and we should treat it like one. If your boyfriend or girlfriend wants to leave you, they should give you two weeks' notice. There should be severance pay, and the day before they leave you they should have to find you a temp."

Accept No-Fault Love the Way We Accept No-Fault Divorce

We could avoid so much heartbreak if each of us would only accept the bittersweet truth about love's demise: *falling out of love is not a betrayal; it just happens. It is useless to assign blame. It isn't your fault, it isn't his fault.* Bonnie Raitt got it right when she sang, "I can't make you love me if you don't."

You are in love with someone, or you aren't. And he is in love with you, or he isn't. There is no Love Potion No. 9. No one can *make* someone love them.

Unfortunately, because we've been taught that "I love you" is a promise and an obligation to love us *forever*, we spend vast amounts of time and energy plotting payback schemes when our lover leaves. It's a waste of your energy, your time, and your life—your one wild and precious life.

Regardless of the circumstances, the demise of a once-passionate relationship is bound to be distressing and heart-rending, but it doesn't have to be full of rancor and revenge. Cope with a break-up in the same spirit of no-fault divorce: it's sad to part, but neither of you are blameless or more at fault than the other. I repeat my advice: the classiest way to deal with a change of heart—yours or his—is to gracefully exit and be generous and compassionate. It is to your advantage to "make nice": an elegant departure leads the way for you to travel on a new and uncluttered pathway to finding a new love.

Can Love Be Rekindled?

I'm often asked if it is possible to "fall back into love" after you have gone through a break-up that was intended to be permanent. According to the love researchers, trying to reignite a relationship is mostly a useless effort—like a slog up a steep mountain on a slippery trail. Apparently, once the brain network that triggers sexual attraction and passion completely loses its connections, it is not likely to get reactivated. Still, if you feel you have the stamina and are willing to make a commitment to reconnecting, you can certainly give it a try.

Making Passionate Love Work for You

11

Replenishing That Lovin' Feeling

It's not surprising that we are fools for love. Most of us have a totally flawed idea about what love is—and isn't—and what we can expect from it. We have been led to believe that shaky and insecure or marginally compatible love affairs make us the most vulnerable to disappointment, hurt, betrayal, desertion, and rejection. But that's just *not* true.

You suffer a wounded heart over love because your misguided hopes and dreams about love can render you helpless to deal with the intensity of passionately loving another person and with the inescapable problems associated with being together. When you don't know the truth about love's ups and downs, your relationships—from dating to being in a partnership—are destined to be high-risk/low-reward experiences.

The good news is that once the "love is blind" stage is over and you miraculously regain your vision you will begin to see him more clearly. Now you can better understand the man you fell in love with, and it is only then that you will begin to experience the depths of the fusion of a passionate love.

In this chapter you'll learn about what goes on behind the scenes in a relationship, how to deal with snags and difficulties that are bound to come up in all relationships, and ways to keep replenishing the love and goodwill between you and the man you love. Most important, I'll help you take an inventory of how your own behaviors and expectations may be affecting the progress of a passionate love or its outcome.

Make the Choice

There is a critical factor in keeping a passionate relationship passionate. You need to acknowledge it is *your* choice to accept or reject the fact that the intense fire of your passion needs loving care to continue to burn brightly. Once you bite off that piece of reality, it becomes possible to work through the problems and enjoy a more committed and realistic passionate partnership.

Consider that emotions in a relationship aren't linear; they are more like a Slinky you put on the edge of a stair to watch where it will go. It rarely does the same thing twice—even though you put it in the very same starting place. Like that slinky, sometimes your relationship moves horizontally, sometimes diagonally, and sometimes it plunks end over end, seemingly out of control. Applying the "Slinky Theory" to your partnership means understanding that your relationship moves in different directions in different circumstances; sometimes you can nudge it in the direction you want it to go and sometimes you can't.

You Say "Tomahto"; I Say "Tomayto"

Let's face it; we are all on our good behavior in the courtship phase of romance. But once we move in together we drop our masks. It is at that point that you learn the truth about love: there is no such thing as a truly compatible couple. Any two people who live under the same roof for any significant amount of time are going to argue. There are irreconcilable differences in the most passionate of marriages, most often about money, sex, in-laws, or child rearing.

Not being consistently sexually or emotionally compatible isn't necessarily a deal breaker, but a mismatch in how to deal with differences (such as when one partner wants to talk it out and the other consistently doesn't, for example) can be deadly. What is important is to recognize that the differences in your personalities will affect the way each of you approaches life and love and the steps you are willing to take toward reconciliation.

Risk Takers versus Non-Risk Takers

One of the less understood and rarely recognized reasons that relationships get off- kilter is an essential difference in your personality traits regarding security versus adventure. Some personalities tend to be high-level sensation seekers and others low-level sensation seekers. At one end of the sensation-seeking continuum are the risk takers—people who love the challenges of competition and get a thrill out of the dangerous—from climbing Mt. Everest to experimenting with drugs. At the other end are the low-level sensation seekers who can't figure out why anyone would want to take such risks. Now, keep in mind that this is a continuum and that most of us fall somewhere in between the two extremes.

The differences in our sensation-seeking personalities can be traced to our brain activity. Studies tell us that people who are most responsive to the release of the kinds of endorphins that signal the "cuddle" hormones tend to be low-level sensation seekers. And thus they are the most able to sustain long-term partnerships. On the flip side, to maintain a buzz, those with thrill-seeking personalities—who tend to feel depressed without regular hits of dopamine and phenylethylamine—are likely to be looking for variety and jump from one liaison to the next.

For a couple, the differences in risk-taking personality traits can turn a plus into a minus or vice versa. There is the electricity of "opposites attract," with a tantalizing sizzle of sexual attraction as well as an energizing learning curve about each other as individuals.

And there may be a downside. Most often, the differences show up in how money should be saved or spent or where to go on vacation—quiet walks on the beach or parasailing from a speedboat—to how much social life is a good thing or an overdone thing. And when it comes to sex, the differences in personalities may emerge as a problem. According to psychologist Marvin Zuckerman, "A person's inherent need for sensation is not necessarily obvious in the early stages of a relationship, when love carries its own thrills. . . . You don't have to be a high-level sensation seeker to enjoy sex. It's when the sex becomes routine that problems occur."

Despite the challenges of balancing stability with variety, there are advantages to being a couple with a mixed level of sensation-seeking traits. For example, low-level-sensation-seeking personalities have a chance to enjoy doing things and going places they wouldn't ordinarily pursue. Like kayaking across Maalaea Bay in Maui or out to the arches at Cabo San Lucas. High-level sensation seekers can benefit from experiencing life at a mellow Norah Jones tempo once in a while while tipping back margaritas and watching the sun go down.

The differences can be perceived as a glass half full or half empty; it all depends on how you hold the glass up to the light.

Keeping "Married" Sex as Spicy Hot as "Singles" Sex

I'll say it for the umpteenth time: for a committed, passionate relationship to stay passionate, *you need to be a passionate lover.* An antiaphrodisiac for passionate sex is having the kind of sex you can set your clock by.

Granted, one of the benefits of being in a committed relationship is that you no longer are dancing to the tune of dating-mating music. But women who are married or in a marriedlike relationship are more frequently mentioning to researchers how rarely they have sex—sweating, satisfying sex that ends with the crescendo of a mind-blowing orgasm. It seems that many women fake "it" for any number of reasons—wanting to assure their partner's ego that he is a sexual hunk or, more simply, to "get it over with" so they can watch a movie, see their favorite TV show, or finish their book. And apparently their partners aren't very demanding either.

Stella Resnick, a well-known therapist from Los Angeles, gave a provocative presentation about sex and monogamy at the Society for the Scientific Study of Sexuality annual meeting in Las Vegas. She pointed out that monogamy, for all its merits, too often results in boring, predictable sex over time. However, she explained, you can avoid those monogamy doldrums—think singles sex. Which means getting the mind-set of a sexy single woman by anticipating the sensual pleasures of going out on a date with the man in your life and looking forward to having great sex with him.

When you think in the mode of "singles sex," Resnick says, "You take the time to select something sexy to wear that not only pleases him but makes you feel sexy and sensuous. You flirt. You are seductive. You feel attractive. What makes sex erotic is that you are playful."

This means you make the effort to make your bedroom inviting and sexy (candles, pillows, nice sheets, and fluffy large guy towels in the bath). You bring out your most seductive ammo—teddies, garters, bustier, slinky lingerie, or black lace thongs with tiny rhinestones spelling out something fun like "You're My Daddy!" across your tush.

"Married sex," Resnick adds "usually occurs in bed at night with the last bit of energy you have left before dropping off to sleep. No wonder it's not imaginative or energetic." But when in a singles mind-set, Resnick suggests that sex doesn't start on a bed, although it may end there. "You get frisky in different places—from the dining room to the car to the floor of the bedroom. Sometimes you are naked, sometimes half-dressed, sometimes only your panties are flung to the four winds."

"Married sex" brings to mind granny T-shirts, jammies with kittens on them, old coffee cups on the dresser, legs that need shaving, and waiting until after the late news to "have sex." Or worse, waking up to the TV droning on in the middle of the night and not remembering if you kissed him good night. I'm exaggerating here to make my point. Sex within a committed relationship has many wonderful things going for it—from trust, to being sexually comfortable with each other to being in a snug and safe environment that allows you to have sex in its hottest and most pleasurable ways.

But no matter how much you and he love each other, having same-old, same-old sex is boring. Obviously not all couples who are in committed relationships are destined to have ho-hum sex. Still, to keep your sex life from snoozing off, you need to shake things up with sexy surprises and put back into play your sexually enticing skills, such as acting and dressing to tempt, attract, and seduce him. (Revisit Chapter 5, "Revealing Your Inner Vixen.")

No, you don't have to be a sex kitten 24/7 (unless you want to), but you do need to pay attention when your sex life needs CPR to keep things alive and interesting.

What About Make-Up Sex?

How does make-up sex fit into the notion of keeping your sex life "interesting"? You know, when a couple has great sex after a fight (not a physical fight but a fight in the sense of a heated disagreement). We've seen it a thousand times on TV and on movie screens. The couple is sputtering words at a rapid pace, screaming accusations, furious with each other. Then, in the middle of their shouting match, they stop, look startled, and immediately begin to tear off each other's clothes. Next scene: they fall on top of each other to land on the floor or the bed or wherever their fury-fueled passion leads them.

Make-up sex's reputation as "great sex" is well earned. After a couple has a knock-down, drag-out shouting match, they're in a physiological state of arousal thanks to a surge of adrenaline. There is increased blood flow through the body, stimulation of the central nervous system, muscle contraction, elevated heart level, etc. They are, well, hot.

Ironically, some of our society's best features—the belief in equality, fairness, and tolerance—can, in the bedroom, result in humdrum sex. Hot sex thrives on power plays, letting your emotions take over, and pulling out all the seduction stops. Given that, it's easy to see why make-up sex is so torrid. (I'm not referring to forced or violent sex: the "act" must have mutual and clear consent and respect for each other's desires and boundaries.)

Despite its ability to produce a heat wave, make-up sex doesn't always work as a way to take a sluggish sex life up a notch. It can't be more than a rare event, or it loses its kick. However, as an unexpected outcome of an argument it can provide a mega-dose of sexual excitement. Studies show that for *some* couples the intensity of reuniting after being angry with each other strengthens their feelings of intimacy.

Avoiding Becoming a Runaway Lover

One of the most earnest reasons to resolve the sexual and other tender issues in your relationship is to avoid the possibility that one of you could become a "runaway lover" because things are too tense. When I say "runaway lover" I'm not talking about the Julia Roberts's *Runaway Bride* movie or women who have gotten cold feet on the eve of walking down the aisle. Don't confuse running away to avoid acting like an adult with the dicey, poignant avoidance emotions that cause someone to move away from the emotional center of being passionately in love.

Although a crisis or a painful argument has passed, wrongs don't right themselves. The hurtful feelings fade in memory but are never really gone—like data on your computer's hard drive—they are recovered in moments of despair or anger. And they are never without cost to the sexual and loving goodwill between you and your partner.

Not dealing with a black cloud hovering over your relationship forecasts a gloomy future for you as a couple. If you encounter a problem that the two of you, with all the good intentions in the world, can't overcome, take steps to deal with what has gone wrong and seek professional help before it gets worse or before things get worse and it becomes late to resuscitate the relationship.

When Commitment Becomes the Elephant in the Room

One of the factors that contribute to unhappiness is when one partner expects and demands commitment before the other person is ready. The person being pressured is a sure-fire candidate for Runaway Loverhood, or at least for becoming frustrated and dissatisfied with the relationship.

If you are the one feeling pressure "to commit" before you feel that is the right thing to do, you are bound to be beyond peeved.

The problem comes from believing that wanting commitment and demanding commitment will get you commitment. Commitment comes from within and has to be freely given. To paraphrase a bit of folk wisdom, "You can lead a horse to water, but you can't make him marry you." Pressure is not only a bad idea; it is counterproductive.

Avoid making assumptions about the other person's motives—accept that you aren't a mind reader. The only way you can come to an understanding of what is going on between the two of you is to have a frank, calm, nonacerbic discussion about the "elephant in the room"—commitment.

The commitment issue may not rest in your relationship. Rather, the roots of the problem may date back to his or your early childhood and adolescent experiences with either rejection or being smothered by someone's anxious love. Essentially, this means that something in the past has contributed to you or to him showing signs of, as psychologist Hara Estroff Marano labels it, a "broken receiver"—a person who has great difficulty receiving love.

In any case, to resolve the issue you'll need to hit the pause button and seek the help of a counselor or therapist to determine if you can go forward or if the relationship has gone as far as you or he can take it.

In any case, to resolve the issue you'll need to hit the pause button and seek the help of a counselor or therapist to determine whether you can go forward or the relationship has gone as far as you or he can take it.

Let Me Count the Ways of Love, Again

Even happy couples have moments when they aren't happy and doubt that they were ever really in love or that they are in love now. Don't impulsively run away at the first (or second even) sign of discord and disagreement. Being passionately in love is never easy. It is intense and involves taking risks; there is sensual energy and loving comfort, and you also have to deal with the slings and arrows that are inevitable in any relationship.

Compare your love relationship to a reservoir. Instead of water, your love tank is full when you are happy and treat each other well, but it begins to empty each time you treat each other badly. The catch is that nobody knows for sure how low the tank is until the last drop of water, i.e. love, is gone. To keep your passion from going dry, you have to replenish love and good feelings in equal amounts—or, better, to exceed the amount of conflicts, tensions, and slights that drain the goodwill between you.

As we talked about earlier, the ratio needed to replenish positive vs. negative feelings is five to one. Again we go to John Gottman, who is renowned for his work on marital stability. He says that what separates contented couples from discontented couples is a healthy balance between their positive and negative feelings and behaviors toward each other. Gottman found as long as there is five times as much positive feeling and interaction between husband and wife as there is negative, the marriage is likely to be stable over time. He claims that when the ratio dips below five to one, the couple is likely to divorce because they were doing far too little on the positive side to compensate for the negative tension. In fact, Gottman says that he can predict with 94 percent accuracy which couples will divorce based on how they deal with conflict.

Make a Whole-Heart Commitment

Given that you have already invested your love, time, and energy in this relationship, wouldn't it be better to agree to disagree on the " small stuff"? Then you can agree on how to find a better way to deal with the usual problems and frustrations of being passionately in love with each other.

For example, can you accept that there is no inherent right or wrong in most personal disputes? There are two or more sides to every issue. Even among researchers, all of whom may be brilliant and pride themselves on their ability to deal with "just the scientific facts," there are differences about what exactly those scientific facts are—and who is right and who is wrong. What counts the most in resolving differences is deciding that your relationship is more important to you than being "right" and making him say "uncle" or keeping score about who won the debate and who lost.

The heart and soul of a passionate partnership is the ability of two people to negotiate any number of issues from bedtime lights being on or off to control of the TV remote control to where to spend Thanksgiving and all of those other unanticipated issues that are bound to come up. This negotiation hinges on loving and a gracious disposition to be kind and generous to each other and, most important, a willingness to be totally present when the two of you are together. Remember Thich Nhat Hanh's teachings: intimacy is being "there" for him. And he for you.

Make a *whole-heart commitment* to your partner and you'll see the small hurts vanish and a deeper level of understanding begin to unfold between you. It will astound you. As Soni told me, "From time to time I remind my partner, Dylan—only half kiddingly—that I might consider murder sometimes, but nothing will ever make me divorce him. I know it sounds strange to hear that as a love message, but he loves hearing me say that because he knows I'm really vowing to be with him no matter what."

There are any numbers of ways couples can express this sense of total commitment to each other. But along with verbal expressions, and above everything else, you have to carve out time for intimacy to continue to flourish. While the universe provides us with an inexhaustible capacity for passion, you have to provide the setting and a willingness (yes, that again) to participate.

12

Just Be You and Love like You've Never Been Hurt

The greatest thing going for you in your quest to find or keep a passionate relationship is *you*. The authentic *you*. In this chapter, we focus on the importance of unmasking who you are and all that is within you—your generosity, the power of your sexuality, and the sweet tenderness of your capacity for loving intimacy. And at the same time, how to avoid the temptation to deep-six the other parts of you that also contribute to who you are: your whiny, controlling, shallow, needy, manipulative, and sneaky secretive side. This is a tough but important task for you to take on because if someone falls in love with your false persona, you have put yourself in an untenable spot. Either you are stuck continuing to wear a mask or you take off the mask and risk losing the man you love. Consider that the most endearing quality you can bring to a passionate partnership is your unique personality and a zest for living to the fullest every single day of your life.

Act Happy, Be Happy

Keep your sunny side up, put your best foot forward, put on a happy face, and smile, smile, smile. You've heard those homilies forever, but as corny as they sound, this advice turns out to be spot on. Studies show that a man is drawn to a woman who has a great smile and an upbeat personality. Actually, any of us are more likely to like someone who is pleasant and has an optimistic attitude than someone who is dour and negative. That is simply human nature.

Taking the "be happy" advice to the lab, researchers are finding that as you act happy your attitude and behavior begin to reflect a more optimistic side of your personality. You will actually begin to be happier. You might like to know that other people's brains are equipped to pick up your smile from yards away, and it is hard for someone not to smile back at you. And a smile is the greatest of all icebreakers.

In a similar way, because expectations can turn into self-fulfilling prophecies—even if you don't completely believe it, picture yourself as a terrific person, one who desires a great job, warm and loving friends, and a wonderful, loving guy to wrap your arms around. The effectiveness of this "Fake it until you make it" approach was verified by researchers at Wake Forest University in Winston-Salem, North Carolina. Students who described themselves as nonextroverts were asked to act like extroverts in class exercises. Turns out they had a great time acting out being assertive, self-confident, and talkative even though they hadn't believed they could do it. Not only could they "fake it," but they found hidden facets of their personality they didn't know they had.

Given all of this, it makes sense to emphasize the positive aspects of your personality and, at the same time, to think about the kind of personality you hope to find in a mate. Witty? Self-confident? Charming? According to that old rocker Mick Jagger, "You can't always get what you want," but if you don't know what you want, you can expect to get (yet another Jaggerism) "no satisfaction."

The Woman in the Mirror

You can't go forward and fully enjoy your zest for love and life until you challenge and put to rest—once and for all—old negative messages that pop out of your mind from nowhere about who you are. Too often, we simmer in a stew of pessimism, focusing on our defects and letting our mind become flooded with the worry that we will never find a relationship that is full of loving and sensual passion.

When you look into a mirror, whom do you see? Like most women, I bet you are able to rattle off ten negative things about yourself without taking a breath. It is one of the vampirelike ego-sucking things most women do to themselves. Our heads are so whacked on weight matters and so full of criticism about almost every part of our bodies that we gloss over the perfectly fine parts of ourselves. In a few words: our body images suck.

The first step to turning off your critical inner judge is to look into a mirror and throw a kiss to yourself —you might begin to even like what you see. It might help to know that others tend to rate you at least one point higher than you rate yourself on a scale of physical attractiveness.

Banishing the Naysayer

There are some people who, for whatever reason, feel the need to pass negative judgment on other people and don't hesitate to let you know what they think. I bet those picky negative folks got an F for communication skills on their report card. Either they are ignorant of the damage they are doing or they think they are "just being helpful" because they love you, or they are having a really bad hair day and are taking it out on you. Maybe they have a hidden agenda to "cut down a tall poppy," or maybe they are just mean! Read Hayley DiMarco's *Mean Girls: Facing Your Beauty Turned Beast* and you will get hiccups remembering the scathing head games girls can play.

We all have had a negative person or two pass judgment on us at some point in our lives. Looking back over my shoulder, I remember a shoe salesman who told me "Your feet are too big, and you can't wear feminine-styled shoes." A real confidence booster for a self-conscious, chunky, and braces-needing fourteen-year-old. After years of no summer sandals I finally came to terms with my nine-and-a-halfs. It took a different salesman—bless his heart—to push the right buttons. I told him in an apologetic voice that I was aware I had "big feet," so I knew I would be limited in my choices. He laughed, looked down at my feet, and said, "Look, everybody has the size feet they are supposed to have. It is ridiculous to say that someone has little feet and someone has big feet. Your feet get you to where you need to go, right? So they are the right size for you."

Your Elevator Talk

It's tempting to believe that there is someone like the Wizard of Oz or something like a magical formula that could help you seamlessly take on the persona of the person you would like to be more like—the person who is drop-dead lovable, desirable, funny, sexy, and—for the icing on the cake— always lucky in love. Unfortunately, wizards are as muddled as anyone else and usually hide behind a curtain of smoke and mirrors. You are better off on your own.

Kathryn, a chef from San Diego, tells me what helped her the most to see herself in a positive light was an exercise I had her do in a workshop called "The Elevator Talk." It goes like this: Describe yourself in forty-five words or less and do it within two minutes. Hit the high notes; skip the low notes. Let's ride up the elevator with Kathryn. "I'm Kathryn. I love to eat and cook, so I'm a chef. Travel is my middle name, and I keep my passport handy just in case. Enjoy good wine and highly charged conversations and sitting outdoors listening to music I haven't heard before." Do you feel you have a pretty good handle on Kathryn's personality? An appealing person you would like to get to know, yes?

I grant you there is a challenge in defining the line between a healthy sense of your attributes and an overly smug arrogant sense of self-worth. There is a fine line between a comfortable amount of self-confidence and an unrealistic amount of self-adoration. Like those irritating people who have self-esteem on steroids—an inflated idea of how smart, good looking, wonderful,and important they are. While it is good to avoid inflating your adorableness, don't deflate it either.

Because, from the other side of the ego-reflecting mirror, if you believe you are inadequate and unattractive, you will attract only men who are among the walking wounded themselves. A worthwhile, mentally healthy man is attracted to a woman who has the same positive qualities he does.

The fine print? The good, the bad, and the everything in between is you being you—distinctively who you are. The better you get at being able to see yourself clearly, the better your chances are of building a foundation of confidence around your assets instead of what you perceive you lack. Nothing is less appealing than a woman who whines about her perceived faults and shortcomings and then pouts about the unfairness of not being as beautiful or as rich as Angelina Jolie or whoever.

Avoid Being a Ditto Girl

Although you can fake it until you in actual fact do feel happier and assertive about life and love, don't fall into the trap of mistaking "faking" it to shore up the positive side of your personality with "faking" the indispensable core of who you are. This includes becoming a Ditto Girl—agreeing to things he says, saying you love sushi when you hate raw fish, going to events that bore you, pouring on compliments that you aren't 100 percent sincere about, and . . . you know the rest of the guy-pleasing drill.

Take Shania's experience, for example. She had a terrific crush on a guy in her office: she was attracted to the way he looked and how he conducted himself. She was thrilled when he asked her out, but less thrilled when over dinner she discovered that he was a rock-solid far-right conservative (and she is a far-left-of-center Democrat). He wasn't shy about stating his opinions on everything from illegal immigration to Hillary Clinton. "We seemed to have so much in common, so I wasn't expecting a radical difference in our political worldview," Shania says. "And that's when I made a judgment call I came to regret. Rather than be confrontational, I reached over and put my hand on his and changed the subject to my favorite movies.

"I really liked the guy—I couldn't see getting into a political debate. Besides, I remembered reading someplace that plenty of couples don't agree on politics and they are happily married—so maybe it wouldn't be a big deal. We went on two more dates, and at some point on each of them he brought up politics. It was getting on my nerves, and I made little noises of disagreement. Mostly, I admit I swallowed my opinions because I was too attracted to him to be direct about how uncomfortable his going on and on made me. Things came to a head when he criticized one of my heroes, Martin Luther King Jr. That was more than I could stand. I told him I was appalled not only by this statement but also by many of his neocon political opinions. He was really surprised, which didn't surprise me, because I hadn't done much more than smile and disagree oh-so-very-gently. He got very quiet. When we got into the car, he told me he could never love a woman with my politics. And it hit me: I couldn't love a man with his politics either! So why was I bothering to pretend that we could have a relationship? What a disaster the whole thing was. I still feel a little ridiculous that I had reverted to *Seventeen* magazine's 'How to Get a Guy' date behavior. Politics matter a lot to me; next time I won't settle for anything less than a liberal Democrat—or maybe a libertarian. Going out with someone who will never be boyfriend material was such a waste of time."

It is understandable that Shania was annoyed with herself for allowing herself to put on a false fluttery-eyed persona to attract him, but it wasn't a waste of time. She learned something about herself—that politics is one of her "big ticket" items that can't be comprised. And at the same time, and equally important, she learned what she won't do in the future just to be in a relationship. Helpful lessons learned for each of us.

Any of us can be on our best behavior early in a relationship—even you. But there is only one way to avoid getting into a fakey relationship: Be your genuine self by exposing your grumpiness in midafternoon, your nitpicky inner Martha Stewart housekeeping expectations, your strong views and opinions about politics and wine, or your couch potato addiction to the Home Shopping Network. You might as well let your true disposition and temperament see the light of day, because faking who you are can't last for long and usually ends badly. The plus is that a man wants a woman to be herself, and it's been my long experience that there is someone who will want you for who you are and for what you have uniquely to offer.

Trust Your Hunches

Despite your more optimistic attitude about love and men, you still fret that you may never have the passionate love you truly desire because you worry you aren't making the right choices. There is another way to navigate around that iceberg and melt it in your wake: trust your hunches.

There isn't just one way to describe and do justice to the meaning of trusting your hunches—your intuition. But a good way to understand it is to picture "intuition" as working in the same way your mind works when you are driving a car—it is called *highway hypnosis*. Your mind is performing tasks without you being consciously aware of the brain's operating processes. You drive a car all the time without a great deal of concentrated thought as to "Why am I doing this?" or "Why should I be in this lane?" or "What do I do next?" You allow yourself to react to the road conditions, other drivers, and staying aware of where you need to exit; all of that is taking place without your being consciously aware of each and every decision you are making. Your brain is processing bundles of information it has been fed in other driving experiences along with classes in driver's ed.

You may not be aware of how much you rely on the nonconscious processes—from simple menu choices to decision making in complex situations—such as the nuances of a passionate relationship. I'm not saying finding a passionate lover is exactly like driving a car, but there are similar nonconscious modes. Remember the love map in your brain? When you meet a man, your brain is computing his attractiveness, his mate potential, and hundreds of other girl-meets-boy details. Research has shown—and this may seem counterintuitive—that in some situations deliberately "over-thinking" about your preferences can confuse you, with your decision possibly not reflecting the best choice for you. In short, you need to give your intuition not only a little credit but a chance to work for you in the mating dance.

Of course, it is always a good thing to gather information about a decision you are faced with, but don't be afraid of letting your gut feelings guide you. You may not be able to articulate rational reasons to justify your decisions. There are times when you just intuitively know what the right choice is, especially when it comes to love and why you are or aren't attracted to a specific man or if you want to develop a relationship or end one. Trust yourself to know what is best for you.

You Are in Charge of Only One Person, and That's Not Him

"He broke my heart!" Making the claim that "My heart is broken because of the behavior of _____ [say, for example, a specific callous guy]" is off the mark. Another person cannot "make" you be heartbroken. You can choose to feel upset and unhappy because he did not act like a kind and loving person. You can wish he acted differently, but you have no control over how he acts. Try it yourself. If you could "make" a person be nicer, wouldn't you do it? If you could make "make" someone like you or—kicking it up a notch—love you, wouldn't you do it?

You can't "make" another person feel what you want him to feel. And nobody forces you to think, feel, or behave a certain way. You are not a victim of people's whims or commands or circumstances. I'm not saying that you can control all situations; of course not. But you alone are responsible for your thoughts, emotions, and actions in relation to that situation. You can create certain alluring scenarios that you think will elicit that "lovin' feeling" response, but you cannot choose his emotion for him. (The pathetic and clueless women on the TV reality show "The Bachelor" make my point.)

You are entitled to feel whatever you want to feel—happy, sad, mad—and then to translate that to any action (within some civil and legal bounds), but you aren't entitled to blame others for what you feel or do. If you choose to be sad because he did you wrong and then rip up every picture of him, that's fine—own the feeling. If he did something you don't like and you choose to be upset and toss marshmallows at him, go ahead. But don't give away the responsibility for your anger or frustrations. You own your emotions. He didn't make you do it.

You may be given a slap on the wrist by your mom, ostracized by your family or peers, or even punished by society if you don't follow certain rules, but nobody else can "make" you do or feel anything. If you give over to another person the power to dictate your emotions—as in "He made me feel terrible about myself," you are giving up way too much of yourself. And that could be the scary beginning of the making of a Stepford wife.

Use your own mind; make your own decisions. And as the familiar advice goes (per the magnet on my refrigerator door):

Dance like nobody's watching;
Love like you've never been hurt ...

Now that's you being *you*.

13

Take-Away Messages

Finding and Keeping a Lasting Love

A friend once told me how love really works. "Falling in love is like the booster rocket that gets us started in defiance of the laws of gravity. When the booster burns out, additional rocket stages have to take the spaceship into orbit. If the only power source is from the booster, the ship will fall back to Earth with a nasty impact. Over the long haul, more powerful engines are needed to provide a stronger power source to last much longer than the spectacular booster if the mission is to be accomplished successfully."

My heartfelt wishes are for you to enjoy the roller-coaster thrills of a newly launched passion and then for you to begin to build the gorgeous complexity of those powerful engines to make it go the distance.

I know the most successful way for you, for me—for any of us—to find and have the sensual and loving intimacy we want and deserve in our lives is to pay attention to what we know for sure about passionate love and put that wisdom to work for us every single day.

Reviewing the Passion Principles

The following are your Passion Principle Cliffs Notes on the various themes and advice about finding and keeping a passionate love that I've woven throughout this book—from why the fireworks of sexual attraction and your revealing your inner vixen are so crucial for lasting love to the torment and the bliss of loving men to coping with the ever-changing emotional landscape of love's journey.

Embrace Your Sensual, Erotic Self

Having a sexy, sizzling connection between you and a fabulous man is the keystone to passionate love. I repeat: if you rate sexual attraction on a scale of 1 to 10—where 10 equals "I want to rip his pants off," 5 equals "whatever," and one equals "nada"—you need to have at least a 6 (better yet, an 8) before pursuing any relationship. And keep in mind that you need to be sexually in tune with him—if not instantly, then definitely before you consider exchanging keys or choosing the china pattern. With real effort and a lot of luck, you might be able to turn the heat up a notch, but because there is so much involved in sexual attraction, it's difficult to do more than that.

I'm not saying that being comfortable with your partner and sharing similar values and goals for your future together aren't important. Of course they are. But no matter how worthy or how "perfect" he seems to be, if some spark of wanton desire isn't ignited within you, he isn't for you. Faking that sexy spark is a wrong turn even if you care for him; it is always disastrous for the relationship. Eventually, the lack of an erotic connection between you erodes the quality of the relationship and it is destined to end badly.

There Is No Secret Express Lane to the Promised Land of Love and Marriage

Don't get caught up in the cultural notion that a "serious" relationship that doesn't end up in marriage is a failure. Jan, a heath technician, reflects back on a relationship that ended and tells me, "Although I didn't marry a man that was very important to me, and although it was poignant and complicated, I still value that relationship because it was meaningful and beautiful for me at the time of my life when I was sorely in need of a loving partner. My only regret is that he didn't choose to stay friends—he is completely out of touch." Jan has the right perspective. It is foolish to cling to the belief that a broken relationship, especially a broken engagement, is like getting hopelessly lost on the way to the only destination that matters: the altar. Having experienced a number of relationships that ended is not evidence of personal failure; relationships end for any number of reasons. You learn what you need to learn and go on.

Be Aware of the Messages You Are Sending

There is a Zenlike saying that when you stop looking, what you are seeking will find you. Be aware of what signals you are sending out to the universe. Avoid sending out messages of loneliness and desperation because they convey a "lonely me" sense of sadness and give men the impression that you are a fixer-upper in need of a serious renovation. Unless he is a talented handyman, he is unlikely to take you up on that offer.

Send positive messages of living a life of abundance, of liking men so much you want one in your life (but at the same time convey that you aren't overwhelmed with urgency to have one). One of the things a man finds most appealing about a woman is when she takes a devil-may-care approach to finding a soul mate. Ask a friend or two that you can trust to give you honest—but not harsh—feedback on how you come across in coed social situations. You may not realize what messages your facial expressions and body language are broadcasting—anything from "stalker chick on the prowl for a husband" to "I'm not really into men."

If you aren't comfortable with asking friends, go to a life coach and ask for some help in putting your inner gal out there in a positive way. Mostly, relax and don't forget to laugh at how funny the whole romantic-love game can be at times.

No One Can Ever Really Know What Is Going On in Someone Else's Head

A corny joke illustrates my point: A man goes into a men's clothing shop. The sales clerk asks him, "Are you thinking of buying a suit today?" Man responds, "Nah, I'm thinking of sex, but I'll buy a suit."

When I told that joke at a conference, the men in the audience howled while most of the women gave me a raised eyebrow or rolled their eyes to the heavens. *Point?* You can set yourself up for a lot of angst by trying to decipher what he is feeling and what he is thinking.

Among the words a man most dreads hearing from us are "What are you thinking?" (For the record, the other one is "We have to talk"; see below.) Unless your lover is exceptionally wise about the ways of women and tells you something to the effect that he is thinking about you constantly and how much he passionately loves you, you are setting yourself up for a fall by trying to interrogate him. Nine times out of ten you won't get much of an answer anyway.

Ironically, what you think is (or should be) causing your partner to feel sad or making him divinely happy often ends up proven otherwise. So lighten up—obsessing over what he thinks is a waste of your valuable energy.

On the flip side, you can drive yourself crazy hoping that your partner will read your mind and figure out what you need and want without having to tell him—a magical trick apparently known only to soap opera's leading men. Give yourself a mental health day: simply tell him.

Accept That Men and Women Talk and Listen on Different Wavelengths

Adding to the miscues of communication between men and women is the way we approach being worried, feeling stressed, or getting bogged down with emotions of being blue—those sad, in-the-dumps feelings. For the most part, women want to talk about their feelings; men prefer to put those emotions in the "vault" and avoid talking about them.

Men say that a woman's "talk" too often turns out to be an excuse for her to give him a negative critique of everything about him that bugs her, from his choice of clothes to his cooking, his sense of humor, his manners, or his lack of culture because he tunes in to a sports event rather than going to see *Mamma Mia!* with her, to what's wrong (in her eyes) with their relationship. How useful is that?

Consider (and I can't repeat this enough) that the man in your life wants so much to please you that he is especially vulnerable to criticism from you, the woman he loves. No matter how nicely you frame your need to "communicate" and clear the air, he is likely to feel you are kicking him to the curb.

The best way for you to be in touch with him emotionally is to stop pushing the same "talk to me" button. Instead, offer him loving hugs—not to initiate sex but to express feelings of being close to him. Of course, talk to him about your worries and rainy-day emotions, but don't make it a big deal as in a dramatic "we have to talk" proclamation. Simply have a conversation, weave in your bullet points, and keep it casual.

Keep in mind that most men have the nanosecond attention span of a mite when it comes to talking or hearing about "our" relationship. One man's lament I heard was this: "Can't we just have a relationship and stop talking about having a relationship?"

For the record—in a BFO (Blinding Flash of the Obvious)—studies show that men use about seven thousand words a day, women about twenty thousand. As comedian Conan O'Brien explains, "A study in the *Washington Post* says that women have better verbal skills than men. I just want to say to the authors of that study: 'Duh.' "

Love Him for His Y Chromosome

You share many personality and psychological traits and dream many of the same dreams as the man you love, but you aren't the same in some fundamental ways. I laughed out loud at the message inside a "girls only" greeting card: "If it has tires or testicles, it's going to be trouble." It has a ring of truth—no matter how thoughtful, kind, attentive, and sexually considerate a man is, or how much he adores you, enjoys cooking Sunday breakfast, goes shopping with you, and loves your family, the Y chromosome is not a mirror image of the X chromosome.

Instead of getting annoyed at him when he acts like a guy, tick off a mental list of what you admire about men: their adventurous spirit, their protective impulses toward us, their enthusiasm and lack of self-consciousness about sex, their refusal to plow the same emotional ground over and over, their easy acknowledgment that not everyone takes a shine to them (and they don't spend any time trying to figure out why!), their robust participation in games of competition and their acceptance of winning and losing, and their ability to forget and forgive their friends' goofs and shortcomings. We can appreciate how more men are displaying qualities that melt us into a love puddle: being gentle and loving lovers and husbands and being wonderfully attentive and patient fathers.

At the crux of a successful, passionate partnership is this simple yet powerful truth: the man in your life wants to be a hero kind of guy that you look up to and adore. Despite some of the downside of the Y chromosome chest-thumping traits, let's be honest: you love it when a man acts like a man.

Speak Well of Your Lover

Too often when women get together—both married and single—we dish about the "man factor" and often say such cynical things about men it makes you wonder why any of us want to be involved or are involved with a man at all. For instance, the topics usually cover the burden we carry dealing with too many housekeeping chores, the too-much-marijuana-or-alcohol factor, his lack of ambition, his boring friends, the neverending drone of sports on TV, too little or too much sex, or the wrong kind of sex.

At the drop of a hat, most of us can produce a long list of our man's shortcomings that inspires our girlfriends to roll their eyes upward to the ceiling, murmuring "uh-huh" affirmations of empathy for the cross we bear.

While we can enjoy the bonding of our beloved sisterhood, we need to stop regurgitating the tired old stories of us as Wonder Women dealing with flawed men. If you really believe that he is seriously flawed, it is time to have a tough-love talk with yourself—find out why you didn't leave when you discovered he was "awful" or why you are still there.

It's OK to complain sometimes about one man in particular or men in general, but be wary of falling into the trap of venting about his flaws to your friends. The problem isn't with the venting per se. It's when you vent about his shortcomings and don't give praise to him where praise is due and your listeners are hearing only a narrow and gloomy side to your relations. As a result, our girlfriends become stern judges, throwing out a sentence to "drop him" or "leave him" when all you wanted was for them to lend you their ears. Or they become a band of cheerleaders, telling you that you are "far too good for him."

The danger is that you can start to believe that you are without fault and there is only one righteous side to this story—your side. That attitude, consciously or not, poisons your loving relationship.

Finally, you are bound to get stuck between a rock and a hard place—damned if you do, damned if you don't. Once you bad-mouth your lover, it is hard to erase what you've said. And after all the bad things you've said about him, you can end up sounding like a love-sopped bimbo when you admit that you don't have any intention of leaving because "you love him." Just be direct and state for the record, "I love _____ even though he drives me nuts sometimes. Thanks for letting me blow off steam—it helps to clear my head. Now, what's going on with you?"

It sounds trite to say "No one's perfect." But trite or not, it is true. Even though the man in your life falls short once in a while, don't we all sometimes?

Allow Each Other Space, Make Waffles, and Get On with It

No matter how deep your passionate intensity goes or how much you finish each other's sentences and anticipate each other's needs, you are each alone as two individuals even in the most intimate relationship. By expecting to sprinkle some magical soul-mate dust over the both of you to become "one," you sabotage the very relationship you desire. Every relationship needs breathing room, and each of you needs a room of your own—both in your mind and private space to live your life, with clear boundaries drawn around it.

In fact, passionate love is a dynamic process of security versus freedom. Almost all of us, from time to time, will face conflicting tensions about love: wanting to be in a cozy cocoon of a relationship and wanting to be free of entanglements; enjoying our solitude but not wanting to be alone. This need for closeness and the need for autonomy are both sides of the same coin.

This means that sharing a passion for each other is a continuous tug-of-war between your need to be intimate with your lover and your need to have a solitary self. This emotional push and pull may never be resolved, but once you acknowledge the dynamics of the process, you can deal with it. It also helps to be aware that this security-versus-freedom tension is never really resolved; it ebbs and flows in every intimate relationship.

If the man in your life says he needs a breather, and you are feeling a tad abandoned, try thinking like a surfer—actually, like a surfer's philosophical relationship to the high and low tides of life. Dorothy Forbes, who writes a column titled "Dear Dora" for the *Taos* (New Mexico) *News*, observes that the reason "surfers are so mellow [is that] they know that about every six hours the ocean will change and there is nothing they can do about it except look forward to the next high tide." What do surfers do when there aren't any gnarly waves in sight? She says, "They go home, make some waffles, and experience the other parts of their life." And she adds, "Relationships are great, but there is this thing that starts with *s* and ends with *pace*, that makes the high tides of relationships that much sweeter." Good advice: when your honey ducks out for a while, get mellow, make some waffles, and get on with your life. Don't take his need for some time to be by himself personally, and remember to pass the syrup.

Before You Vow to Forsake All Others, Take a Moment

Marriage is one of the most misunderstood relationships undertaken in the name of love. Love is an emotion, but marriage is a legal contract and a traditional social, religious, and economic institution. Love may last, but there are no guarantees. You can't predict how you'll feel in a year, let alone over a lifetime. Yet we are expected to make marriage vows to be together "forever." The reason is that marriage is as much about the vows of commitment to society, church, and family as it is about your personal vows to keep on truckin' through the hills and valleys of being married, no matter what.

Sadly, some couples, after the rosy glow of postwedding days fades, find they are swallowed up by marriage, stuck with partners who are only intermittently the people they bargained for. Their marriage may not be a death spiral into a black hole, but it is not what they had hoped and dreamed it would be.

Consider whether marriage, as it is traditionally defined, is the kind of partnership you want to enter into—not what others think you *should* want but what you *want*. Think about it. Is it marriage, and if so, what kind of marriage? Or is it a live-in partnership? Or is it being together but living in two different places? How do you feel about Katharine Hepburn's idea of the perfect relationship, in which "You live next door to each other and visit frequently"?

Consider how your sexual desires are fulfilled in this relationship before deciding to marry and take the long walk down the aisle—and then, gazing deeply into the eyes of your beloved, pledging to forsake all others. You will be promising that he will be the only man you will ever—that is *ever*—have sex with, "till death do you part." That is a very long time indeed.

Pick a Decent Mate

It's true—you can't tell your heart whom to love. But you can use your head to narrow the field. To up the chances of being happily together—in some form that suits you—pick a partner that you can passionately love and passionately love a decent person—one who is honest, loving, understands and controls his temper, expresses affection without being nudged, has a funny bone that tickles yours, and whom you adore because he is a wonderful human being. A man who treats everyone with respect and kindness and who is at peace with himself; a man about whom you are proud to say, "He's my guy." A Scottish (I think) proverb speaks to having the good sense to find a partner that is a decent person and not to marry based on winding-down bio-clocks or desperation or insecurity: "Never marry for money; it's cheaper to borrow."

Passion Doesn't Come with a Never-Changing Guarantee

As snuggly and wonderful as being romantically in love feels, it doesn't come with a guarantee of the "happily ever after" ending of love's fairy tales. Our passionate love emotions change from time to time, our wealth and travel hopes and dreams change, our bodies change (and not usually for the better); everything around us is constantly changing. Despite our good intentions, intimate relationships are difficult to achieve and sustain. Too little time and money, too much working stress, and family issues can weaken a couple's feelings of commitment and sexual intimacy. At some point, every couple's love relationship arrives at the crossroads of consolidation or disillusionment.

The truth is, it is written in the stars—a reflection of human nature—that the pyrotechnics of sex in even the sexiest relationship will flicker and smolder and then reignite again. If you can face the reality that the high drama of your early-on over-the-top sexual desires for each other are bound to ebb and flow, and if you both can agree to resolve disappointments and differences, you can have the best of all worlds—an erotic bond in a relationship that offers friendship, adventure, and contentment.

Last Thoughts: Passion Is the Rainbow's Pot of Gold

As we come to the close of our journey together, I want to remind you of the key messages we began with and then encourage you to take these— along with all of the preceding messages—into your heart.

- Being passionately in love rocks your world like nothing else because it is an erotic, sensual, vulnerable, volatile, euphoric emotion that hijacks the soul, the mind, and the body. Whatever the conscious or unconscious forces that trigger a passionate spark within you—one that sexually and emotionally draws you to a special man—this much is sure: a craving for passion and an intimate partner is a universal human longing. Every culture recognizes some form of the need to love deeply and be loved in return. But far from the global village, in your little corner of this world, your passionate emotions are unique to you.

- Being passionately in love with a partner you like, trust, and respect means experiencing the sweetness of romantic love and the spicy-hotness of being sexually in tune with each other. It is a relationship worth seeking, and it is one worth keeping.

- Embrace yourself as the passionate woman you are, and allow yourself to be connected to a sensual and loving man in a way that is sexy, gritty, full of risks, good times and bad timing and feels like finding a pot of gold at the end of love's rainbow.

My fondest wish for you is for you to be ready when a passionate love comes a-knockin' at your door. And it will.

Resources

Books

One of the best books on sexuality and sensuality is Kim Cattrall's (yes, *that* Kim Cattrall). Easy-to-digest information based on solid research, plus it is beautifully, sensually, and erotically illustrated. *Sexual Intelligence* (New York: Bullfinch Press, 2005). Makes a great gift too.

Two books you *must* keep by your bedside are: *Passionate Hearts: The Poetry of Sexual Love* (Novato, CA: New World Library, 1996) edited by Wendy Maltz, and *Intimate Kisses: The Poetry of Sexual Pleasure*, also edited by Wendy Maltz (Novato, CA: New World Library, 2003). These anthologies of sexual poetry are erotic, unique collections of poems that inspire and celebrate healthy sexual intimacy. Maltz's website is worth the visit: HealthySex.com.

A Natural History of Love by Diane Ackerman (New York: Random House, 1994). A unique take on why we fall in love the way we do, written in Ackerman's rapturous prose.

The New Science of Intimate Relationships by Garth Fletcher (Oxford: Blackwell Publishers, 2002). Readable and solidly researched.

Intimate Relationships by Sharon Brehm, Rowland Miller, Daniel Perlman, and Susan Campbell (New York: McGraw-Hill Higher Education, third edition, 2002). Basically a college reader but an excellent book for anyone interested in science-based information about all aspects of romantic relationships.

She Comes First: The Thinking Man's Guide to Pleasuring a Woman (New York: Regan Books, 2005) and *He Comes Next: The Thinking Woman's Guide to Pleasuring a Man* (New York: Regan Books, 2006), both by Ian Kerner. Practical answers to the questions asked most frequently about sex. Also see Kerner's website—it's great; he is spot on with his advice: IanKerner.com.

Sex Is Not a Natural Act by Leonore Tiefer (Boulder, CO: Westview Press, second edition, 2004). Tiefer is a well-known feminist and sex researcher and writes from a wide-ranging perspective.

The Heart & Soul of Sex: Making the ISIS Connection by Gina Ogden (Boston: Trumpeter, 2006) A wonderful book that connects women's sexuality and spirituality and gives us an insightful look into women's emotions about sex and love. Gina's other book is also an eye opener: *Women Who Love Sex: Ordinary Women Describe Their Paths to Pleasure, Intimacy, and Ecstasy* (Boston: Trumpeter, 2007). Also see her companion educational video, titled *Women Who Love Sex: Creating New Images of Our Sexual Selves.* Her website is at womensspirit.net.

Knock-Your-Socks-Off Sex by Shannon Mullen (New York: Crown Publishers, 2004). This is a lot of fun to read and is full of great tips and common sense.

The Passion Prescription: Ten Weeks to Your Best Sex— Ever! by Laura Berman (New York: Hyperion, 2005). An all-around solid and readable guide about how to let yourself enjoy, as she says, "the best sex ever."

The Good Girl's Guide to Bad Girl Sex by Barbara Keesling, Ph.D. (New York: M. Evans and Company, Inc., 2001). Another good book on what to do and how to do "it." Besides, who doesn't want to be a bit sexy-bad?

Betty Dodson's many books and films are jazzy, fun, and edgy. You gotta love Betty! Her website, bettydodson.com, is chock-full of self-help sexy information and materials.

Prime: Adventures and Advice on Sex, Love and the Sensual Years by Pepper Schwartz (New York: Collins, 2007). A very appealing memoir with terrific advice about the ups and downs of postdivorce sex life as a "seasoned" woman.

Finding Your Perfect Match by Pepper Schwartz (New York: Perigee, 2006). Advice about how to determine whether someone is a potential match before getting deeply involved.

The Soul of Sex: Cultivating Life as an Act of Love by Thomas Moore (New York: HarperCollins Publishers, 1998). Also see *Soul Mates: Honoring the Mysteries of Love and Relationship* (New York: HarperCollins, 1994).

Good practical advice is found in Sol Gordon's *"How Can You Tell If You're Really in Love?"* (Cincinnati, OH: Adams Media Corporation, 2001).

Jealousy by Nancy Friday is the best book on jealousy ever. (New York: Perigord Press Book, 1985). All of her other books starting with *My Secret Garden* are essential reading. Check out her website: nancyfriday.com

The Four Agreements by Don Miguel Ruiz (San Rafael, CA: Amber-Allen Publishing, 1997). I reread some of it every day.

The Pleasure Zone: Why We Resist Good Feelings and How to Let Go and Be Happy by Stella Resnick (Los Angeles:

Conari Press, 1998). Opens the doors to enjoying more pleasure and joy in our lives.

The Erotic Mind by Jack Morin (New York: HarperCollins, 1995). A fresh and insightful perspective on love and sex.

Put Your Big Girl Panties On and Deal with It! by Roz Van Meter. Warm, down-to-earth, and full of tips you can use. Roz says, "Don't get your panties in a twist. It's time to grow up, take over your own life, and get what you really want!" (Naperville, IL: Sourcebooks, Inc., 2007). Roz will be your new best girlfriend! I love this book.

Erotica

Good Vibrations. Both online shopping and retail (stores in San Francisco and Berkeley). Online: Extensive, well-managed, and colorful archives of toys, vibrators (don't miss the Vibrator Museum), books, audiotapes, and videos; lists of the bestselling in each category. Quality extras: news, columnists, newsletter, and sex trivia outreach events, philosophy. A must visit at goodvibrations.com. Also visit selfserve.com, a sexuality resource center.

Sinclair Intimacy Institute. Some of the most tasteful adult sex education "better sex" materials available. The "Better Sex Guide to the Kama Sutra Set" is especially good. At bettersex.com.

Candida Royalle's *Femme Productions.* Well-produced erotica materials that speak in a woman's voice and also offer couples-oriented sexually explicit films. CandidaRoyalle.com.

Check out tantrasource.com for information about a form of sex that many people practice for its mind-body-spirit connections.

Eve's Garden; also includes the Berman Center Intimate Accessories Collection. evesgarden.com.

Websites

eDiets.com

For expert advice on sex, love, relationships (I know, this is an unlikely site). Its cadre of experts is outstanding, and the articles are concise and informative.

sexscience.org

Society for the Scientific Study of Sexuality. Information about research and researchers in sexual science.

aasect.org

American Association of Sexuality Educators, Counselors and Therapists. It can provide a list of certified sex educators, counselors, and therapists where you live.

sexualhealth.com

Provides sexuality information, online counseling, and referrals.

siecus.org

SIECUS (Sex Information Education Council of the United States)

nsre.sfsu.edu

National Sexuality Resource Center

A clearinghouse for current sex issues, sexuality research, and social policy.

Hite-research.com

Hite Research International, Shere Hite's resource center.

gender.org

Gender Education and Advocacy (GEA) deals with gender-variant people's needs and issues.

ptpinc.org/products_Dawna_Markova.html

A great source for Markova's work.

References

The bricks and mortar that built this book came from many sources over time. I can't list them all, but some of the key text references include:

Diane Ackerman's work is my inspiration, especially *A Natural History of Love* (New York: Random House, 1994). Her unique lush prose and depth of understanding about love, sex, and passion led me down the path to writing this book.

Helen Fisher's books and many articles have been invaluable, specifically *Why We Love: The Nature and Chemistry of Romantic Love* (New York: Henry Holt & Co., 2004).

Intimate Relationships by Sharon Brehm, Rowland Miller, Daniel Perlman, Susan Campbell (New York: McGraw-Hill Higher Education, third edition, 2002).

The Handbook of Sexuality in Close Relationships, edited by John H. Harvey, Amy Wenzel, & Susan Sprecher (Mahwah, NJ: Lawrence Erlbaum Associates, 2004).

The New Science of Intimate Relationships by Garth Fletcher (Oxford: Blackwell Publishers, 2002).

Dimensions of Human Sexuality by Curtis O. Byer and Louis W. Shainberg (Dubuque, IA: WCB Brown & Benchmark Publishers, fourth edition, 1994).

Sexuality and Gender in Society by Janell L. Carroll and Paul Root Wolpe (New York: Addison Wesley Publishers, 1996).

The Continuum Complete International Encyclopedia of Sexuality. Edited by Robert Francoeur and Raymond Noonan (New York: Continuum, 2004). Search the encyclopedia at kinseyinstitute.org/ccies/globaltrends.php

Notes

Introduction

Ironically this belief about compatibility: See Garth Fletcher, *The New Science of Intimate Relationships* (Oxford: Blackwell Publishers, 2002). Fletcher says, "The belief that high similarity between partners is good for relationships is a popular one . . . and indeed, it is an argument that one finds frequently expounded both in academic textbooks and pop-psychology treaties. The empirical evidence, however, is less than convincing." (135).

What is overlooked: See Willard Gaylin and Ethel Person, eds., the classic *Passionate Attachments: Thinking About Love,* (New York: Free Press, 1988).

For example, Pepper Schwartz, a sociologist well known for her research: Pepper Schwartz quoted in David Leonhardt, "Computing the Mysteries of Attraction," *New York Times*, nytimesee.com (accessed March 29, 2006). For the Internet matchmaker's sexual chemistry efforts, see Lori Gottlieb, "How Do I Love Thee?," *Atlantic Monthly*, March 2006.

Helen Fisher, an anthropologist at Rutgers: Helen Fisher quoted in David Leonhardt, "Computing the Mysteries of Attraction," *New York Times*, nytimes.com (accessed March 29, 2006). For a review of Internet match-making, see *Albuquerque Journal*, "Have You Discovered Your Chemical Match?," February 12, 2006, 6–8.

I was reading Wendy Lee's "Lover's Duet": Wendy Lee in *Passionate Hearts: The Poetry of Sexual Love*, ed. Wendy Maltz (Novato, CA: New World Library, 1996), 60–61. Also see another piece I often read from the same book, "Purple Is the Color of the Longing" by David Steinberg, 32–33.

Chapter 1

I drowned in the fire: From a wise but unknown source.

You have to have passion: See *The Handbook of Sexuality in Close Relationships*, ed. John H. Harvey, Amy Wenzel, and Susan Sprecher (Mahwah, NJ: Lawrence Erlbaum Associates, 2004). Also Garth Fletcher, "Love and Other Emotions" in *The New Science of Intimate Relationships*, 76–102.

Why do we spend so much: For a comprehensive review of theories, Garth Fletcher, "Three Theoretical Planks," in *The New Science of Intimate Relationships*, 21–102, and for sociobiology see Timothy Perper's still-relevant book, *Sex Signals: The Biology of Love* (Philadelphia: ISI Press, 1985).

There is, however, a loophole: For how sexual desire and arousal fits into the "mating-baby" game, see Roy Levin, "Sexual Arousal—Its Physiological Roles in Human Reproduction," *Annual Review of Sex Research* 16 (2005):154–189.

Scientists are discovering that love activates: For what sets off the chain reaction of love, sex, and passion, see Helen Fisher, *Why We Love: The Nature and Chemistry of Romantic Love* (New York: Henry Holt & Co., 2004). Also see the scholarly work of Eva Illouz, "The Lost Innocence of Love: Romance as a Postmodern Condition" in *Love & Eroticism*, ed. Mike Featherstone (London: Sage Publications, 1999).

You might as well face it: See Paul Mermelstein's research reported in "In Brief," *Health*, September 2005, 156. Also see Kim Cattrall, *Sexual Intelligence* (New York: Bullfinch Press, 2005), 80.

In one study, oxytocin: Hannah Bloch and Sally B. Donnelly, "The Love Chemicals," *Time*, February 15, 1993, 51.

While there is some overlap: See "In Brief," *Health*, September 2005, 156, and Kim Cattrall, *Sexual Intelligence*, 69–78.

In fact, people who have just: Catherine Shu, "Insights," *Psychology Today*, November/December 2005, 30.

As you move forward from the roller-coaster ride: See Helen Fisher's reference to "cuddle chemicals" in Kim Cattrall, *Sexual Intelligence*, 83, and Sandra Latifi, "Love Chemicals," *Albuquerque Journal*, August 2006, 8.

Given the sheer number of men: Census Bureau reports in the *Wall Street Journal*, August 30, 2006, D1.

Chapter 2

She seemed to be speaking: Mary Oliver, "The Summer Day," PoemHunter.com (accessed May 14, 2007).

Thomas Moore, the author of *Soul Mates*: Thomas Moore, *Soul Mates: Honoring the Mysteries of Love and Relationship* (New York: HarperCollins, 1994).

Despite the billion-dollar marriage marketplace: Kate Zernike, "Why Are There So Many Single Americans?," *New York Times*, December 12, 2007. Also see "What's New?," Report for Better Scientific Research on Courtship (accessed September 18, 2002).

Yet the Census Bureau reports: Census Bureau statistics reported by Christine Whelan, author of *Why Smart Men Marry Smart Women* (New York: Simon & Schuster, 2006) in *Wall Street Journal*, November 3, 2006, w13.

There has been a steady increase: Nancy Wartik, "The Perils of Playing House," *Psychology Today*, July/August 2005, 42–52.

Although the romantic fairy-tale books: See Christine Whelan, *Wall Street Journal*, November 3, 2006, w13.

Thich Nhat Hanh, a Zen Buddhist monk: Thich Nhat Hanh, "Do You Have Time to Love?," from his book *True Love* (New York: Shambhala Publications, Inc., 2004), Belief.com. (accessed October 2, 2006).

It's not that devoting time: For dilemma of friends versus family, see psychologist Daniel Kahneman's work reported in *Psychology Today*, January/February 2005. He says, "People report being happier when they are with friends than when they're with a spouse or child."

Moving beyond list making: Sir Isaac Newton's First Law of Motion in "Newton's Laws of Motion," *The Physics Classroom*, Glenbrook. K12.il.us (accessed November 19, 2006).

Follow in the path of poet Dawna Markova: "I Will Not Die An Unlived Life" by Dawna Markova in *I Will Not Die An Unlived Life: Reclaiming Purpose and Passion* (Newburyport, MA: Redwheel Weiser and Conari Press, 2000), 1. Also see her website, ptpinc.org.

Chapter 3

Each of us carries in our mind: Helen Fisher, *Why We Love: The Nature and Chemistry of Romantic Love*, 118–21. For John Money's concepts, see Kim Cattrall, *Sexual Intelligence*, 60,75.

Before Sandra Bullock knew much: Sandra Bullock quoted in news.yahoo.com. (accessed February 14, 2007).

You share a sense of humor: See Sol Gordon, *How Can You Tell If You're Really In Love?* (Boston: Adams Media Corporation, 2001).

Chapter 4

News anchor Brian Williams says: Williams quoted in *O*, June 2005, 58.

That rush of "love" chemicals stimulates: Helen Fisher, *Why We Love: The Nature and Chemistry of Romantic Love*. And for how the brain chemistry of attraction sets off a sexual spark, see Laine Bergeson, "The Big Organic O," *Utne Reader*, May–June 2005, 20–21.

To be blunt: your nose leads: Carlin Flora, "Does Love Make Scents?," *Psychology Today*, September/October 2004, 40–58.

These pheromones play a role: Etienne Benson, "Pheromones, in Context," *Monitor on Psychology*, APA On Line, apa.org/monitor.html (accessed December 7, 2004), and F. Bryant Furlow, "The Smell of Love," *Psychology Today*, March/April 1996, 37–42.

It could work for us: See Etienne Benson,"Pheromones, in Context."

Take, for example, you and: McClintock's study reported in Sanjay Gupta, "The Chemistry of Love," *Time*, February 18, 2002, 69. Also see Carlin Flora, "Does Love Make Scents?," 40–58, and F. Bryant Furlow, "The Smell of Love," 37–42.

Just in case, if you are using: See Carlin Flora, "Does Love Make Scents?," 48–50.

Based on those notions of pheromones: Erox study reported in Etienne Benson "Pheromones, in Context."

It may sound a bit creepy: See Garth Fletcher, "Selecting Mates and Relationships," 69–193, especially the section "Searching for the Ideal Mate" in *The New Science of Intimate Relationships*, 170–93.

For example, men claim they: See Kevin Kniffen's study reported in "Evolution and Human Behavior," *Health*, January/February 2005, also William F. Allman, "The Mating Game," *Mysteries of Science, US News &World Report*, July 19, 1993, 65, 67, 82. And for additional studies on women's perception of men's mate potential and masculinity, see James Roney and Dario Maestripieri's work reported in Don Baldwin, "Women Like Men Who Like Kids, Study Finds," *Albuquerque Journal*, May 10, 2006, A9.

This "Breadwinner Fast Track" legacy is changing: See W. Bradford Wilcox and Steven L. Nock's study in "What's Love Got to Do With It? Equality, Equity, Commitment and Women's Marital Quality," *Social Forces* 84, no.3 (March 2006):1321–45. They claim that the single most important factor in a woman's marital happiness is the emotional engagement of the husband. They also found that women who report the highest level of happiness with their marriages are those who have husbands who earn the lion's share of the family income so the women don't have to work outside the home. Even among women who support egalitarian ideas—that is, those who think that men and women should both earn income and should share house-work equally, there is greater marital happiness when the husband earns 68 percent or more of the family income. Regardless of what married women say they believe about gender, they tend to have happier marriages when their hus-bands are good providers—provided that he is also emotion-ally engaged. For more about women being drawn to men of means, go to sugardaddies.com

Psychologist David Buss surveyed: David M. Buss, *The Evolution of Desire: Strategies of Human Mating*, revised and expanded edition (New York: Basic Books, 2003).

Researchers believe men are attracted: Jennifer Connolly, Virginia Slaughter, and Linda Mealey, *The Journal of Sex Research* 87, no.1 (February 2004):5–15. Also see K. Singh, "Adaptive Significance of Waist-to-Hip Ratio and Female Physical Attractiveness," *Journal of Personality and Social Psychology* 65 (1993): 293–307.

Although it is disputed: For a dissenting view on WHR as being consistent over time, see Jeremy Freese and Sheri Meland's "Seven Tenths Incorrect: Heterogeneity and Change in the Waist-to-Hip Ratios of *Playboy* Centerfold

Models and Miss America Pageant Winners, *The Journal of Sex Research* 39, no. 2 (May 2002): 133.

Check out his hands: For information on the personality types designed by Helen Fisher, see "Have You Discovered Your Chemical Match?," *Albuquerque Journal*, February 12, 2006, E6, and Lori Gottlieb, *Atlantic Monthly*, March 2006.

It seems that the ratio of finger lengths: See Lori Gottlieb, "How Do I Love Thee?," *Atlantic Monthly*, March 2006, 58 and 65, and "The Finger of Destiny," based on researcher Mark Brosnan's work, in "Indexing Science: Report on Digit Ratios of Academic Staff," *Atlantic Monthly*, March 2005, 50.

Women make very good use: Dario Maestripieri quoted in Abigail W. Leonard's "How Women Pick Mates vs. Flings," Special to *Live Science*, Jan. 2, 2007. Livescience.com/health/070102_facial_features.html (accessed May 13, 2007). Also see Don Babwin's "Fatherhood at First Sight: Women Can Spot Good Dads by Their Faces," livescience.com/health (accessed May 13, 2007). The classic study by Elizabeth Cashdan, "Cads vs Dads," reported in William F. Allman, "The Mating Game," 70. And for more on how women react to men's photos, see *Time*, August 5, 2002, 68.

Researcher Dr. Shinsuke Shimojo: Shinsuke Shimojo quoted in "In Brief," *Health Magazine*, April 2004, 111.

"Love," she says, "is a commingling of body and soul": Hannah Block quoted in "The Chemistry of Love," *Time*, February 18, 2002, 72.

Chapter 5

We say we crave great sex: Kathleen McGowen, "Sex Shockers," *Glee Magazine*, GleeMagazine.com (accessed March 20, 2007).

As a woman, you have a brain that is organized: Shawn McKee "Men, Women: Mars & Venus or Different Wiring," ediets.com (accessed August 10, 2006).

To let yourself "have sex": Barry Komisaruk, Carlos Beyerk-Flores, and Beverley Whipple's *The Science of Orgasm* (Baltimore: John Hopkins University Press, 2006), and Cindy M. Meston, Roy J. Levin, Marca L. Sipski, Elaine M. Hull, and Julia R. Heiman, "Women's Orgasm" in *Annual Review of Sex Research: An Integrative and Interdisciplinary Review XV* (2004): 173.

I was walking around the exhibits: See Badmimi .com.

What counts is what turns you on: For how we constrain our sex play, see John Ince, *The Politics of Lust* (Amherst, NY: Prometheus Books, 2005). He explains: "Most of us have a very narrow erotic repertoire, a short sequence of erotic acts that varies minimally from day to day, partner to partner. We fear any form of sexual experimentalism or originality. While we seek out the new in movies, books, food, travel, fashion, computers, and so on, our sexual expression remains bland and repetitive" (p. 335).

In fact, women report wanting: See Kathleen McGowan, *Glee Magazine*, 2007.

For example, 27 percent of women: Reported in *Self*, December 2006, 40.

First of all, check in: An issue might be oral contraceptives. See Anne Davis and Paula Castano, "Oral Contraceptives and Libido in Women," *Annual Review of Sex Research: An Integrative and Interdisciplinary Review XV* (2004): 297–320.

Some scientists claim that the roots and shoots: Laine Bergeson, "The Big Organic O," *Utne Reader*, May/June 2005, 20–21.

Chocolate contains phenylethylamine: Michael Castleman,"Health LifeStyles and Spas," *Utne Reader*, January–February 2005.

There are pluses and minuses of pharmaceutical: See Hazel Curry, "After Reports That 'Pink' Viagra Has Gone Limp, Doctors Are Exploring Cognitive Methods of Rekindling Lost Lust in Women," *The Observer*, March 30, 2003, observer.co.us (accessed May 12, 2007), and Lori Brotto's "Female Viagra: Innovations in the Science of Women's Sexuality," *NUVO*, Summer 2003, 104–106 (plus some very cool illustrations). Also Leorore Tiefer, a well-regarded feminist sex researcher, "The Pink Viagra Story: We Have The Drug, But What's the Disease?," *Radical Philosophy*, no. 21 (September/October 2003): 2–5 (this is a terrific article, and not much has changed since she published it).

As writer Sally Kempton put it: Kempton quoted in sallykempton.com/home.html (accessed April 12, 2007).

Researcher Pat Koch and her colleagues: Patricia B. Koch, Phyllis K. Mansfield, Debra Thurau, and Molly Carey, "Feeling Frumpy: The Relationship Between Body Image and Sexual Response Changes in Midlife Women," *The Journal of Sex Research* 42, no. 3 (August 2005): 215–23.

Still, according to researcher Ann Bridges: Research reported in "Women Aroused as Quickly As Men," paper presented at the Canadian Sex Research Forum Annual Meeting, Ottawa, Sept. 30, 2006. Meredith Chiver's study reported in Michele Bryner, "For Women, A World of Turn-Ons," *Psychology Today*, July/August 2005, 26. Also see Lisa Featherstone, "You, Me and Porn Make Three," Psychology Today, September/October, 2005, 83–87.

Why not find a guy friend: Laura Sessions Stepp, *Unhooked: How Young Women Pursue Sex, Delay Love and Lose at Both* (New York: Riverhead Books, 2007).

As a gender, you are pretty much wired: Elizabeth G. Pillsworth and Martie G. Haselton,"Women's Sexual Strategies: The Evolution of Long-Term Bonds and Extrapair Sex," *Annual Review of Sex Research: An Integrative and Interdisciplinary Review XVII* (2006): 59.

Chapter 6

Men can get crazier about love: See David Zinczenko, "What Makes Men Fall in Love?," *Men's Health*, http://Health.yahoo.com/experts/menlovesex (accessed March 21, 2007). Also, for more insight into men's take on love and such, see a charming collection of essays in *Men Tell Stories of Love, Commitment and Marriage*, ed. Cris Knutson and David Kuhn (New York: Bloomsbury, 2005).

As psychologist David Buss points out: Buss quoted in William F. Allman, "The Mating Game," *Mysteries of Science, US News & World Report*, July 19, 1993, 65. For the mating games we play, see David M. Buss, *The Evolution of*

Desire: Strategies of Human Mating. revised and expanded edition (New York: Basic Books, 2003).

Studies show that men have two: Louanne Brizendine *The Female Brain* (New York: Broadway Books, 2006).

It isn't helpful, however, to measure a man's sexual: See researcher Kim Wallen's work in *Sexual Appetitive, Desire and Motivation: Energetics of the Sexual System*, ed. Walter Everaerd, Ellen Lann, and Septhie Both (Amsterdam, Netherlands: Knaw Edita, 2001), 154. Reviewed by Cynthia Graham, in *Journal of Sex Research* 39., no. 2 (May 2002): 154–5. Also see Kim Wallen, "Ovarian Influences on Female Development: Revolutionary or Evolutionary?," *Behavioral and Brain Sciences* 21 (1998): 339–340.

Most surveys about sex: Robert Roy Britt, "Why Men Report More Sex Partners than Women," posted on Livescience.com/othernews/060217_partners (accessed March 20, 2007).

Most guys know more about: Ian Kerner quoted in his website, iankerner.com (accessed February 10, 2007).

What many women fail to understand: Erick Janssen, Harriet Vorst, Peter Finn, John Bancroft, "The Sexual Inhibition (SIS) and Sexual Excitation (SES) Scales: Measuring Sexual Inhibition and Excitation Proneness in Men," *The Journal of Sex Research* 39, no. 2 (May 2002): 114–26.

For evidence, we travel: This shaky bridge study has been widely reported for decades. The original article is D. G. Dutton and A. P. Arron, "Some Evidence for Heightened Sexual Attraction Under Conditions of High Anxiety," *Journal of Personality and Social Psychology* 30 (1974): 510–17.

Variety for a man is the spice of sex: See Jack Morin, *The Erotic Mind* (New York: HarperCollins, 1995).

Ian Kerner, the sex therapist: Kerner quoted in Rachael Combe, "The Sex Problem No One Talks About," *Self,* January 2007, 118.

Let's peel that onion: See Ziauddin Sardar's study in Laine Bergeson, "The Big Organic O," *Utne Reader*, May–June 2005, 20.

But "andropause," the gradual: For more information about testosterone and men's sex drives, see Isadore Rosenfeld, "Do You Need a Testosterone Boost?," *Parade Special Issue on Men's Health,* June 18, 2006, 6.

Worrying about a recent less-than-stellar: See Michele Weiner-Davis, "Sex Drives: His and Hers" from divorcebusting.com/a_sex_drives.htm (accessed January 30, 2007).

Psychologist Regan Gurung says: Regan Gurung, "The Male Brain: See How it Runs," *O*, April 2006.

Chapter 7

In all passionate relationships: Meredith Maran, "If You Like Me, Back Off!," *Health*, October 2005, 135–40.

Both of you should have an equal: For more about avoiding overstepping each other's boundaries, see Pat Love, *The Truth About Love*, (New York: Fireside Books, 2001), and Jeffrey B. Rubin, "Stand Back from the Rope," *O*, March 2005, 193–5.

As Don Miguel Ruiz, in his elegant book: Don Miguel Ruiz, *The Four Agreements: A Practical Guide to Personal*

Freedom (San Rafael, CA: Amber-Allen Publishing, 1997), front flap.

The grating truth may be: See Greg Behrendt, Liz Tuccillo, and Laureen Monclich, *He's Just Not That Into You: A Newly Expanded Edition: The No-Excuses Truth to Understanding Guys* (New York: Simon Spotlight, 2006).

In addition to paying close attention: Credit to Nina Utne for information about Heart Math, in *Utne Reader*, November–December 2004, 56. And for more about HeartMath, go to heartmath.org.

But let there be spaces: Kahlil Gibran, *The Prophet* (United Kingdom: Senate Press Limited, 2002), 15–16.

Chapter 8

Jealousy and envy are often spoken: For more about how jealousy plays in our relationships, see Sharon Brehm, Rowland Miller, Daniel Perlman, and Susan Campbell, *Intimate Relationships* (New York: McGraw-Hill Higher Education, Third Edition, 2002, 283–93. Also see "Jealousy" in Curtis Byer and Lois Shainerg, *Dimensions of Human Sexuality* (Madison, WI: Brown and Benchmark, 1994), 95–100.

Psychologist Harriet Lerner offers this advice: See Harriet Lerner, *Fear and Other Uninvited Guests* (New York: HarperCollins, 2004).

Nando Pelusi, a psychologist in private practice: See Nando Pelusi quotes in "Jealousy: A Voice of Possessiveness Past," *Psychology Today*, July/August 2006, 64–5.

Women have been known to do wacky: For some of women's revenge strategies, see Leanne Shaptin, *Was She Pretty?* (New York: Sarah Crichton Books, 2006).

Deeply felt and acted-out jealousy: For more about the destructive side of jealousy, see "Conflict and Violence" in Sharon Brehm et al., *Intimate Relationships*, 283–93.

Granted, your emotions derive: See Garth Fletcher, *The New Science of Intimate Relationships*, 224–6.

Chapter 9

Take, for instance, how authors: Cathi Hanauer and Dan Jones quoted in Gina Bellafante, "His and Her Books Tattle on Marriage," *New York Times*, June 13, 2004, Section 9-2.

There is a paradox about: For more about surveys and information about cheating, see aamft.org/familes/consum erupates/infidelity.asp (accessed March 30, 2007).

When we are intimate: See Sharon Brehm et al., *Intimate Relationships*, 297–307.

They build a wall of secrecy: The "wall of secrecy and window of intimacy" concept derived from Shirley Glass, "Infidelity" from aamft.org/consumerupdates/infi delity.asp (accessed March 30, 2007). Also see her book, Shirley Glass, *NOT "Just Friends": Protect Your Relationship from Infidelity and Heal the Trauma of Betrayal* (New York: Free Press, 2003).

As author Scott Peck warned us: Quote from Scott Peck, *The Road Less Traveled Quotes Calendar*, March 19, 2000.

So let's take a step back: See Diane Shader Smith, *Undressing Infidelity: Why More Wives are Unfaithful* (Cincinnati, OH: Adams Media, 2005), and Christina Nehring's review of Diane Shader Smith's book and the topic of cheating in "Fidelity with a Wandering Eye," *Atlantic Monthly*, July/August, 2005, 135–41.

A Player Personality: See Benedict Carey, "A Highly Inflated Version of Reality: Researchers Challenge Notions About What Drives the Chronic Liar," *Los Angeles Times*, March 3, 2003, latimes.com/features/heath (accessed March 6, 2003).

*Note***: An old study about menstrual:** From William F. Allman, "The Mating Game," *Mysteries of Science, US News World Report*, July 19, 1993, 69.

Whether a relationship is three weeks: For the most insightful piece on cheating—it still holds up and is a must read—see Frank Pittman, *Private Lies: The Betrayal of Infidelity* (New York: W. W. Norton, 1989).

Specifically, you can create: See Brehm et al., *Intimate Relationships*, 297–306.

Chapter 10

Love is blind only to the extent: Concepts related to arrows and "inputs" and "outputs" based on early work of Martin Blinde, *Choosing Lovers: Patterns of Romance, How You Select Partners in Intimacy* (New York: Glenbridge, 1999).

As psychologist Elaine Hartfield observed: Hartsfield quoted in Hannah Block and Sally Donnelly, "The Love Chemicals," *Time*, February 15, 1993, 51.

Some people may crave intimacy: Joel B. Bennett, "Research Notes on Chaos: Dynamic Relational Systems and the Mandala Principle," in *Time and Intimacy, A New Science of Personal Relationships* (New York: Lawrence Erlbaum Associates, Inc., 2000), 115–18.

Chapter 11

One of the less understood: For more about high and low sensation seekers, see Marvin Zuckerman, *Sensation Seeking and Risky Behavior* (Washington, DC: American Psychological Association, 2007). Zuckerman is also quoted in "Cupid's Comeuppance," *Psychology Today*, September/October 2000, 46.

But no matter how much you: For more about married sex and libido, see Esther Perel, *Mating in Captivity: Reconciling the Erotic and the Domestic* (New York: HarperCollins, 2006).

Still, to keep your sex life: See Gregory Berns, *Satisfaction: The Science of Finding True Fulfillment* (New York: Holt, 2005). He explains that what lights up the brain more than pleasure is the *pursuit* of pleasure.

How does make-up sex: Raphael Calzadilla, "The Science Behind . . . Make-up Sex!" In http://eDiets News, *Sex and Relationships* (accessed April 29, 2007).

This commitment issue may not rest in your relationship: For "broken receiver," see Hara Estroff Marano's "Let The Love Shine In," edit.socm/new/print. #632101 (accessed September 28, 2006).

As we talked about earlier: John M. Gottman, *Why Marriages Succeed or Fail* (New York: Simon & Schuster,

1994), and J. M. Gottman and R.W. Levenson, "Marital Processes Predictive of Later Dissolution: Behavior, Physiology and Health, *Journal of Personality and Social Psychology* 63(1992): 221–33.

Make a Whole-Heart Commitment: See Lydia Dykes Talmadge and William C. Talmadge, *Love Making: The Intimate Journey in Marriage* (St. Paul, MN: Syren Book Co., 2005).

Chapter 12

The effectiveness of this: See 'fake it until you make it" research reported by Liz Vaccariello, *Prevention*, December 2006, and a quote from Ovid: "Pretend to what is not, so when the passion is over, you'll become, in truth, what you are studying to be."

When you look into a mirror: For more about how others rate you see, Carlin Flora, "Mirror Mirror: Seeing Yourself as Others See You," *Psychology Today*, May/June 2005, 54–8.

There is another way to navigate: Richard Wiseman, *The Luck Factor* (New York: Miramax, 2004).

But a good way to understand: For more about "highway hypnosis," see Hara Estroff Marano's column "Can You Trust Your Intuition?" in ediets.com/news (accessed August 29, 2006).

Dance like nobody's: Quote from Mark Twain at http://inspiring-thoughts.tripod.com/dance.html (accessed August 2, 2006).

Chapter 13

Dorothy Forbes, who writes a column: Personal interview based on her column "When the Going Gets Tough . . . Make Waffles," *Taos News*, March 15–21, 2007, C8.1

As snuggly and wonderful: For how sex in a relationship changes, see Carl A. Ridley, Rodney M. Cate, Dawn M. Collins, Amy L. Reesing, Ana A. Lucero, Michael S. Gilson, and David M. Almeida, "The Ebb and Flow of Marital Lust: A Relational Approach," *The Journal of Sex Research* 43, no. 2 (May 2006): 144. Also see W. Bradford Wilcox and Steven L. Nock, "What's Love Got to Do With It? Equality, Equity, Commitment and Women's Marital Quality," *Social Forces* 84, no. 3 (March 2006):1321–45. The authors claim the single most important determinant of a woman's marital happiness is the emotional engagement of her husband. A wife cares most about how affectionate and understanding her husband is and how much quality time they spend together as a couple.

It is written in the stars: See *The Handbook of Sexuality in Close Relationships*, ed. John H. Harvey, Amy Wenzel, and Susan Sprecher (Mahwah, NJ: Lawrence Erlbaum Associates, 2004), and Christina Nehring, "Of Sex and Marriage," *Atlantic Monthly*, December 2006, 124–7.

Index